Add-a-Line

Continuous QUILTING Patterns

Janie Donaldson

American Quilter's Society

P. O. Box 3290 • Paducah, KY 42002-3290
www.AQSquilt.com

Located in Paducah, Kentucky, the American Quilter's Society (AQS) is dedicated to promoting the accomplishments of today's quilters. Through its publications and events, AQS strives to honor today's quiltmakers and their work and to inspire future creativity and innovation in quiltmaking.

Editor: Helen Squire
Graphic Design: Lynda Smith
Cover Design: Michael Buckingham
Photography: Charles R. Lynch

Library of Congress Cataloging-in-Publication Data
Donaldson, Janie
     Add-a-Line: continuous quilting patterns/ by Janie Donaldson.
      p. cm.
      ISBN 1-57432-795-X
     1. Quilting--Patterns.   I. Title.
     TT835 .D0664 2002
     746.46'041--dc21
                       2002008655

Additional copies of this book may be ordered from the American Quilter's Society, PO Box 3290, Paducah, KY 42002-3290, or online at www.AQSquilt.com.

Dedication

This book is dedicated to the loving memory of my mother, Mary Jane Jennings. As the oldest daughter, she spent many hours as a seamstress, re-designing patterns and making clothes for 10 siblings. Integrated into the continuous line designs presented in this book are her experiences, thoughts, and words of wisdom gained as a professional fashion designer. She passed on her knowledge to me and my two sisters. Thank you, Mom, for having the patience and time to teach us the principles of good design.

Thank you, Mary Edward, Helen Squire and the staff at AQS, for your ingenious computer work and diligence in putting my book together.

Introduction

Add-a-Line is written and designed for quilters who love to use a pantograph. Quilting layouts that are made with these continuous line designs can be pre-determined easily and sewn accurately. Even though the single line idea is a beginner technique, lines have been added to "jazz it up." Also, by re-setting the width of the lines that are in multiples, you can achieve wide to narrow borders.

I have given you a variety of themes and ideas, from modern to traditional, that will speed your work along. Choose the skill and complexity of the design you want. Whichever one you choose – from one to four lines – these designs have an inherent beauty. They work well for all-over quilting and special borders, as well as for individual blocks. The designs can be separated, run singly, or spaced as you like.

Have fun and stay a stitch beyond the rest.

Janie Donaldson

Contents

ONE FOR THE MONEY
Single Line Quilting

Add-A-Line Continuous Quilting Patterns ⟶ *Janie Donaldson*

placement diagram

placement diagram

The little dots represent an area where we can add jewels, sequins, beads or additional thread in a sparse satin-stitch design. This is often called *jetting* when done on a longarm quilting machine.

The normal spacing for pantograph patterns is ¾" between the rows. This measurement is only a guideline, as personal preference and individual quilt size are always factors.

placement diagram

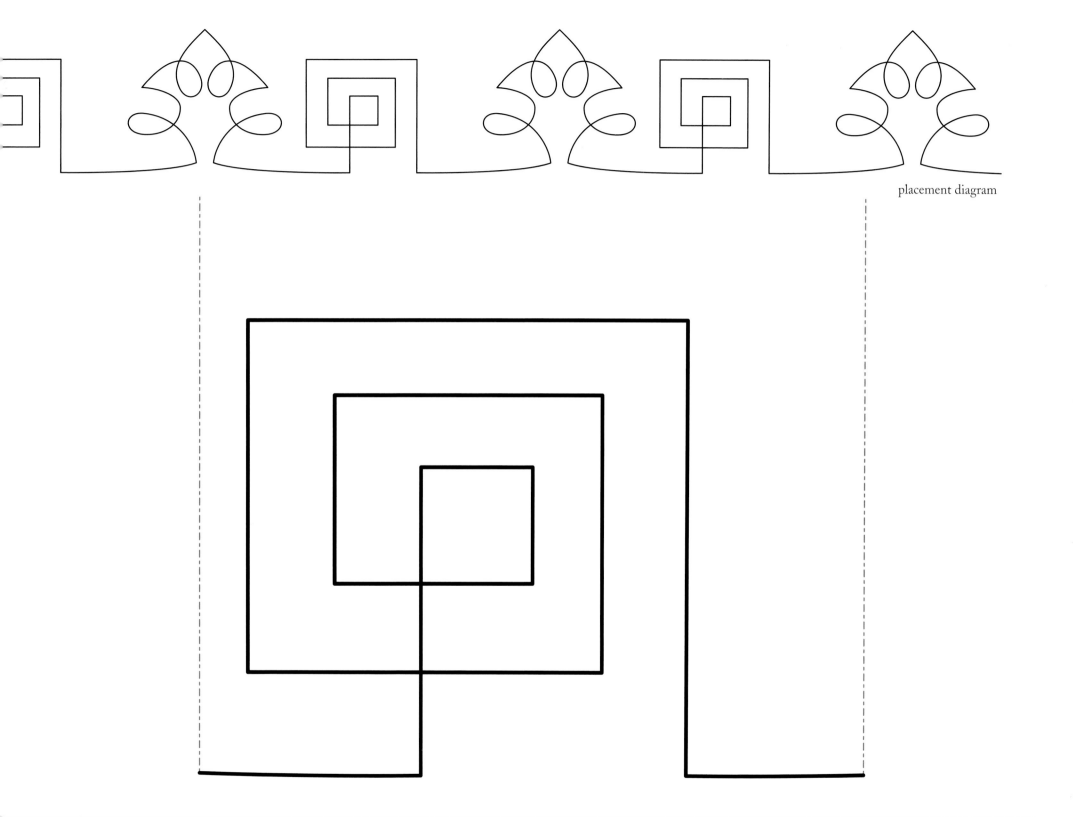

placement diagram

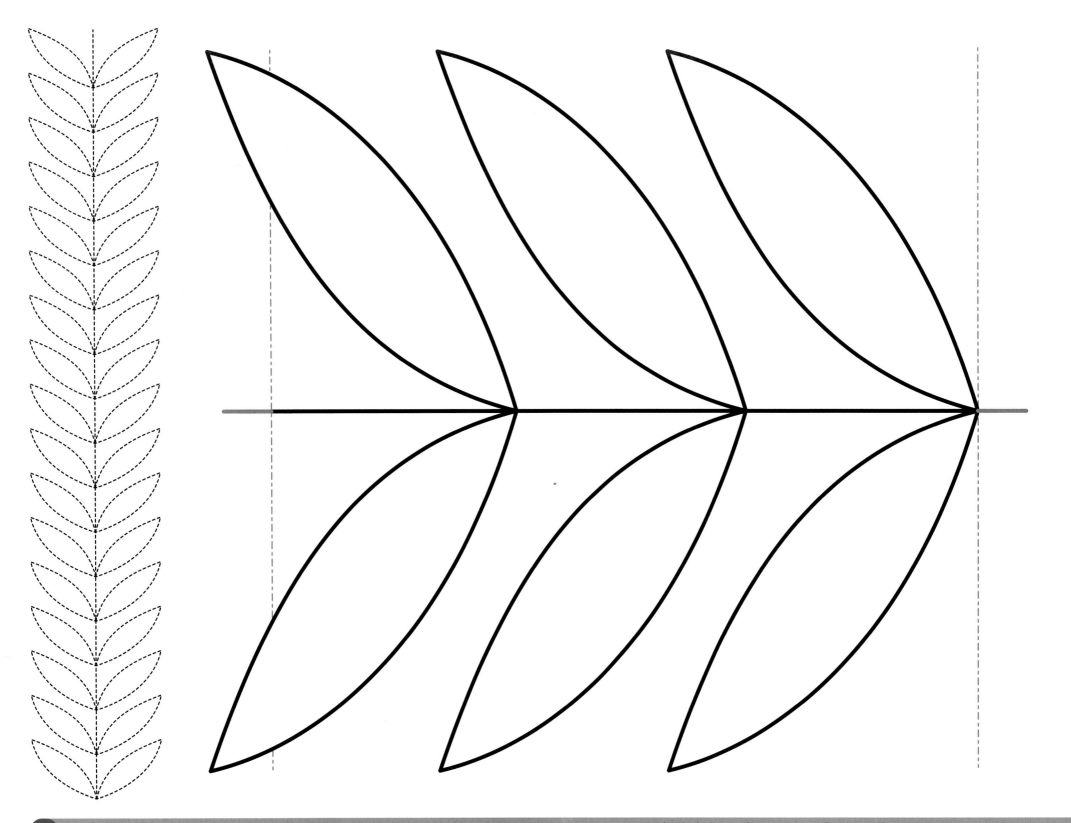

placement diagram

placement diagram

*Red lines indicate quilting areas that require a change of direction.

placement diagram

As you start into the butterfly, do the accent marks on the inside of the first wing, then the outside outlines of the same wing, then the antenna, and as you do the second wing, do the outside on this first and then the inside accent mark, just the reverse.

placement diagram

Add-A-Line Continuous Quilting Patterns ⬝ *Janie Donaldson*

placement diagram

placement diagram

CONNECT HERE

placement diagram

CONNECT HERE

Tulip & Button Block – 8"

Add-A-Line Continuous Quilting Patterns ➤ *Janie Donaldson*

Add-A-Line Continuous Quilting Patterns — *Janie Donaldson*

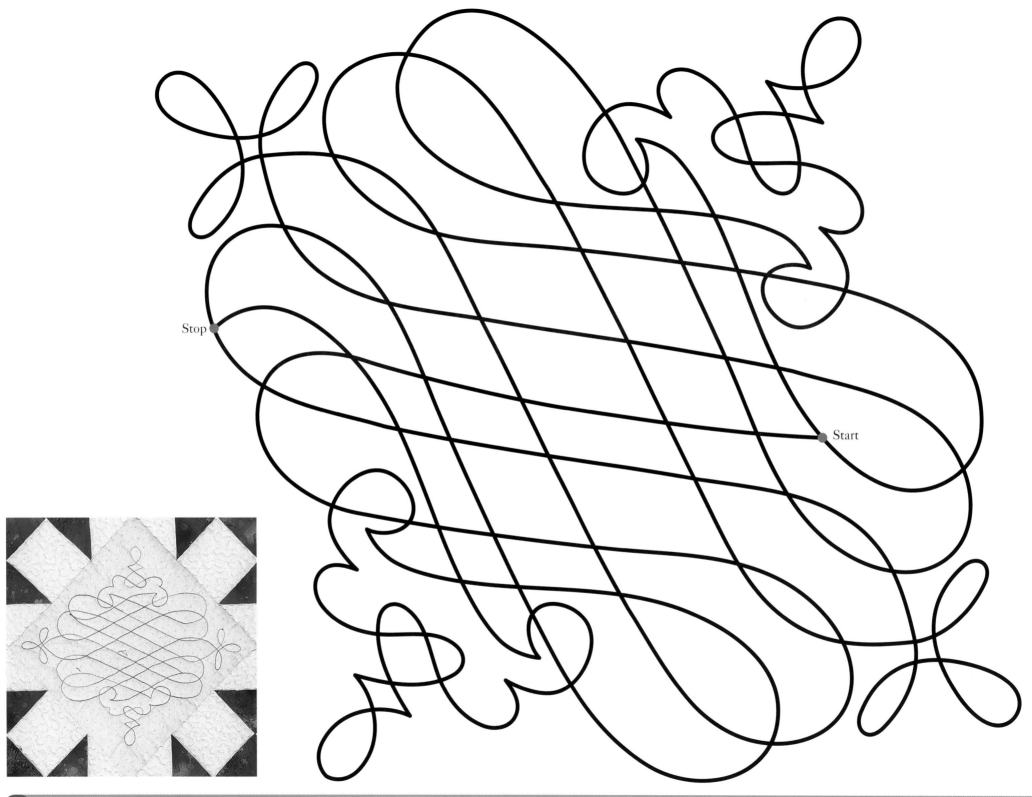

Stop

Start

TWO FOR THE SHOW

Double Line Quilting

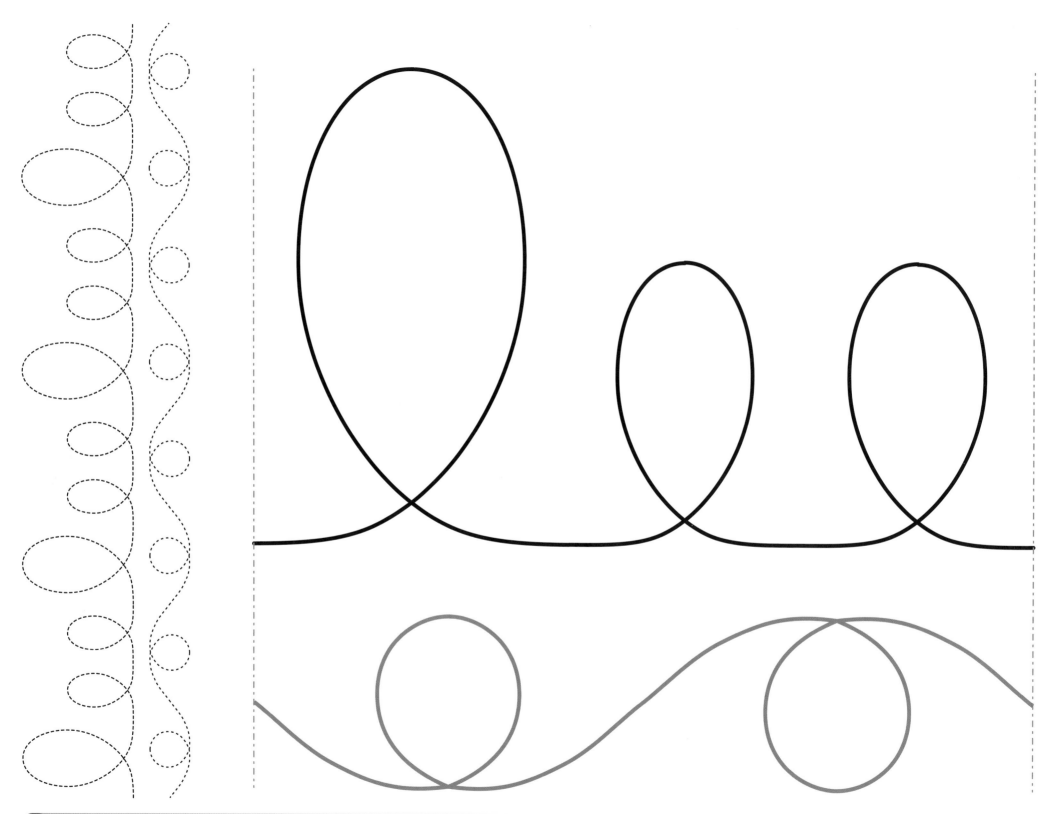

Add-A-Line Continuous Quilting Patterns — *Janie Donaldson*

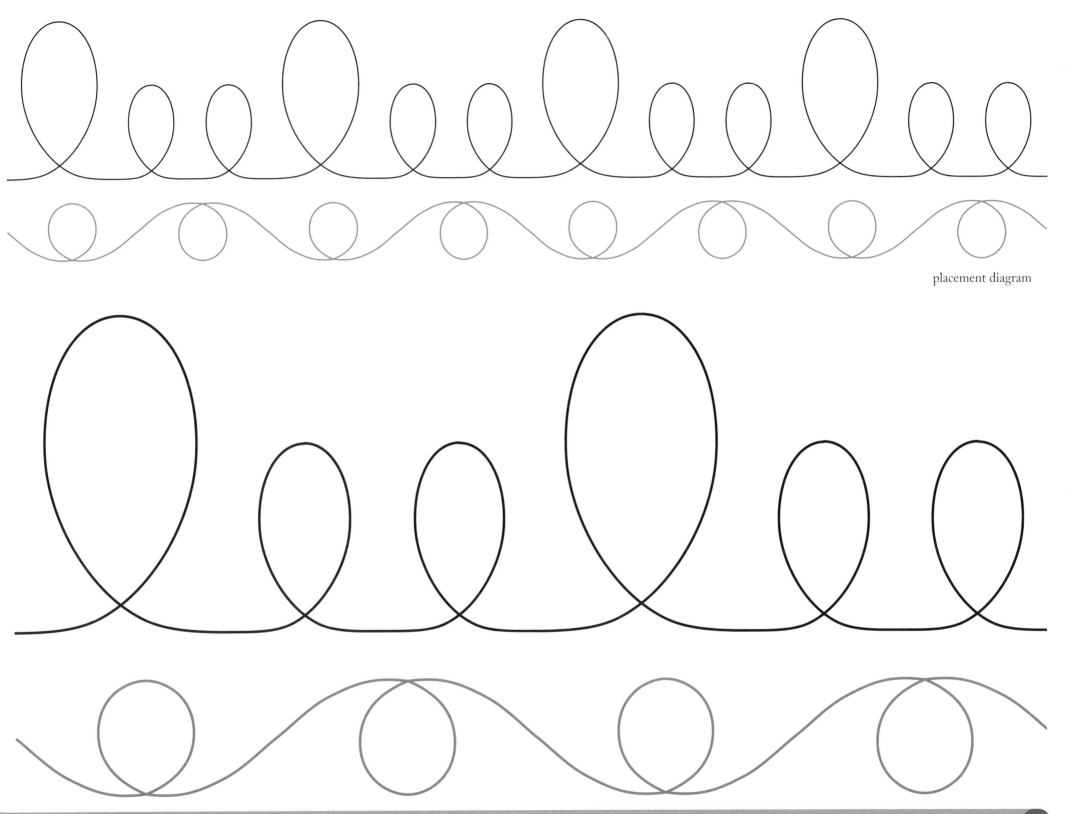

placement diagram

placement diagram

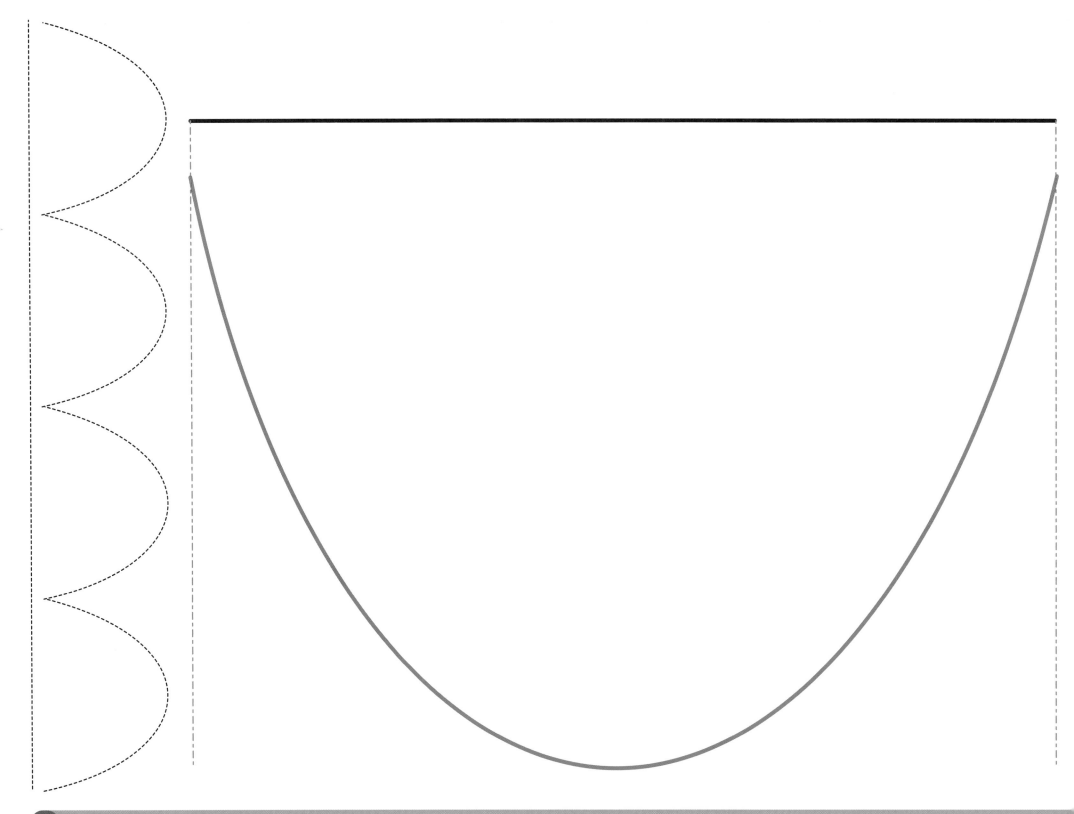

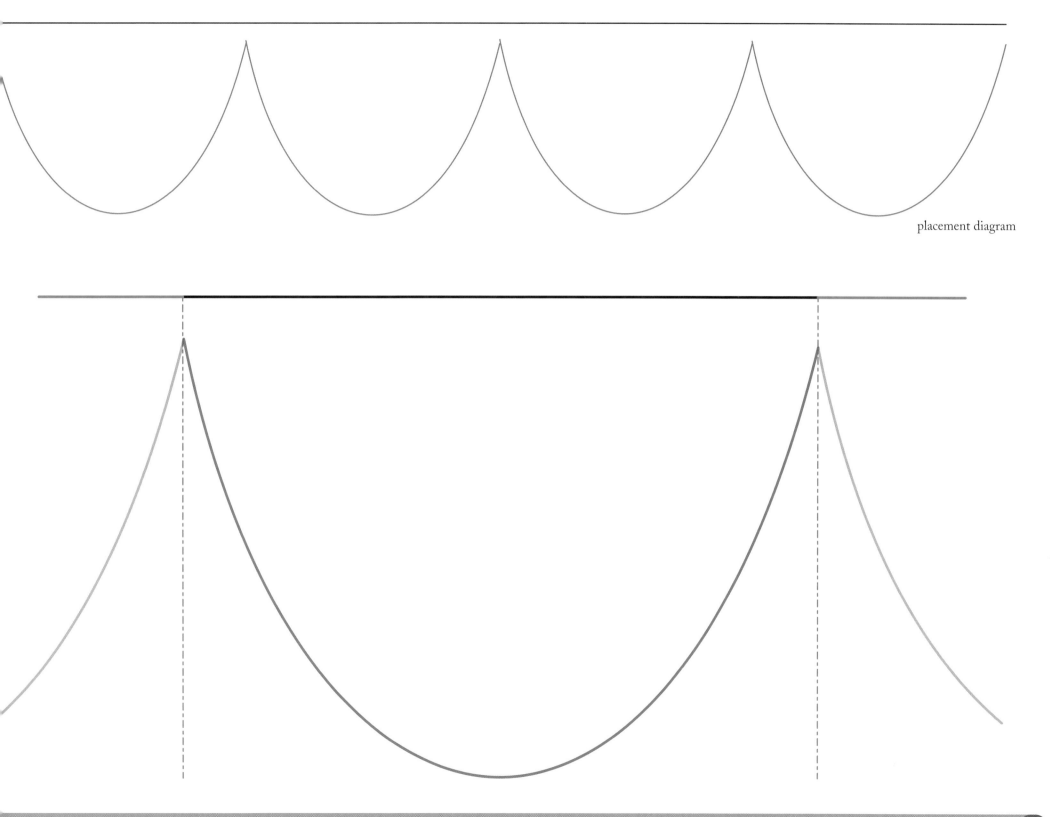

placement diagram

placement diagram

placement diagram

Add-A-Line Continuous Quilting Patterns — *Janie Donaldson*

placement diagram

placement diagram

*Red lines indicate quilting areas that require a change of direction.

Add-A-Line Continuous Quilting Patterns — *Janie Donaldson*

placement diagram

Add-A-Line Continuous Quilting Patterns ⟶ *Janie Donaldson*

placement diagram

placement diagram

THREE TO GET READY
Triple Line Quilting

*Red lines indicate quilting areas that require a change of direction.

placement diagram

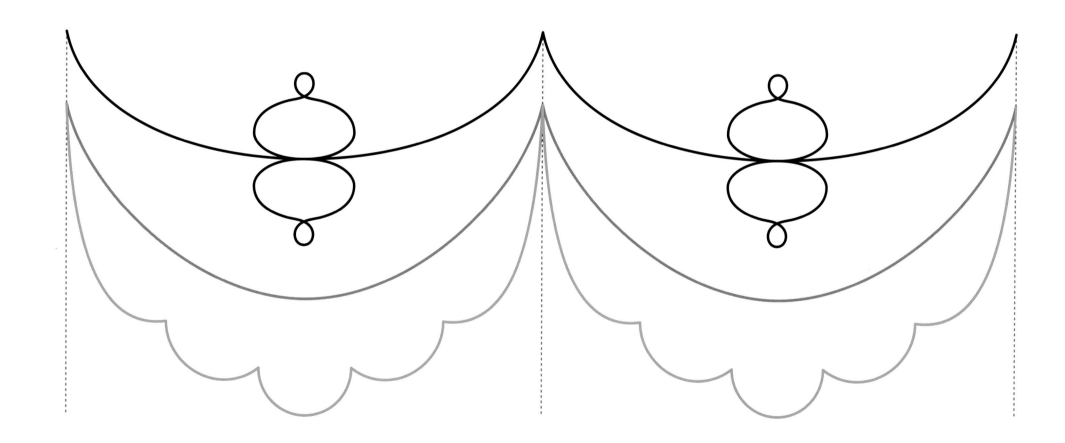

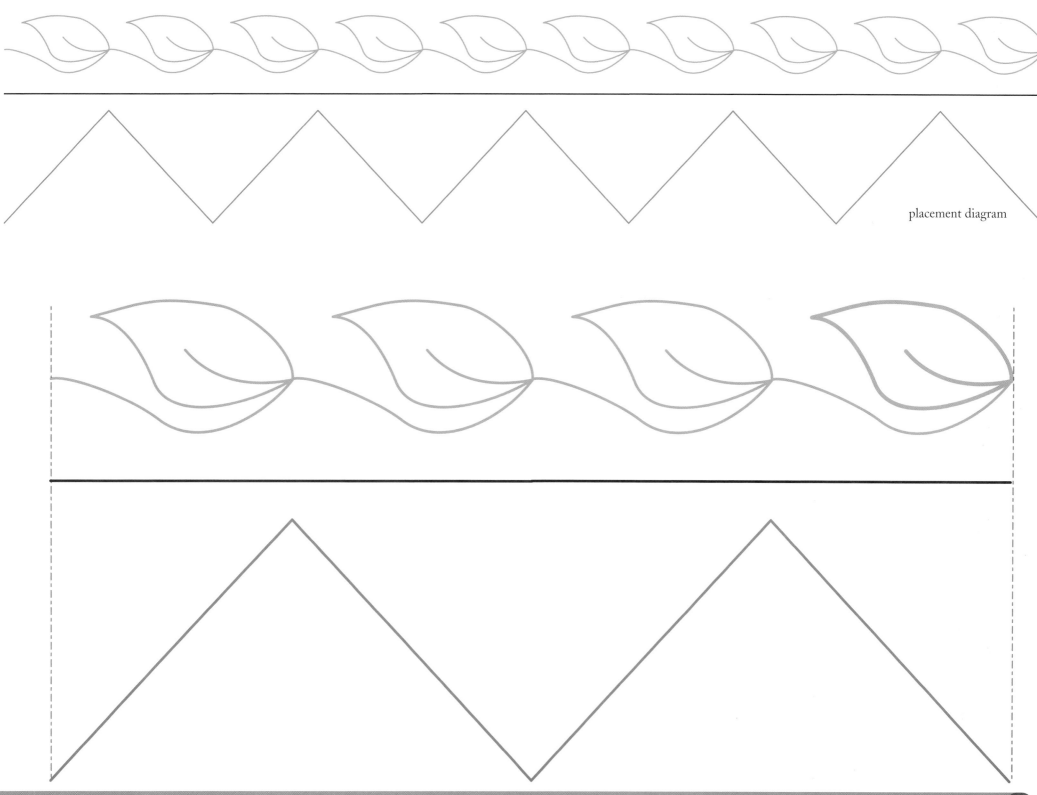

placement diagram

placement diagram

placement diagram

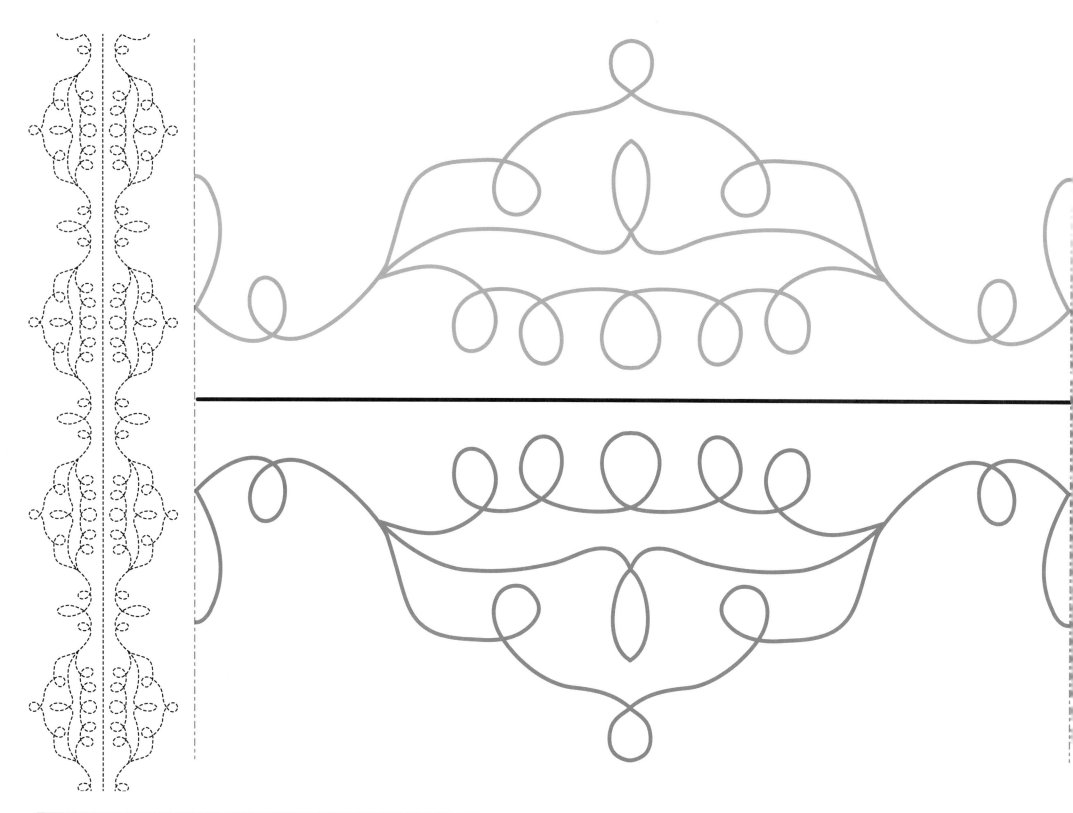

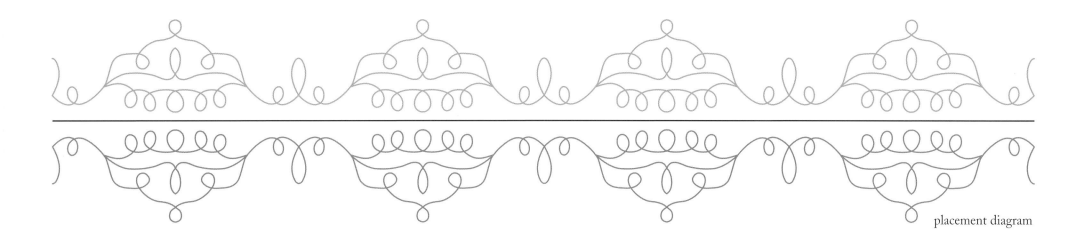

placement diagram

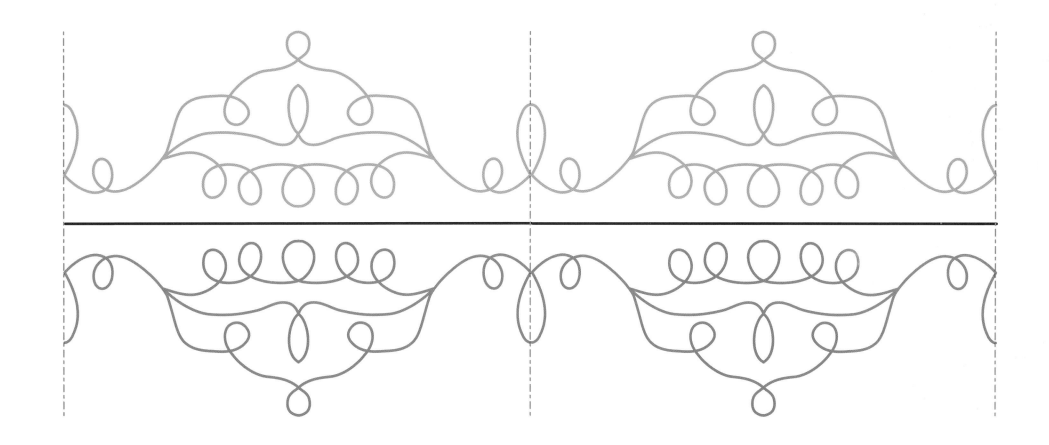

placement diagram

Add-A-Line Continuous Quilting Patterns — *Janie Donaldson*

placement diagram

Add-A-Line Continuous Quilting Patterns — *Janie Donaldson*

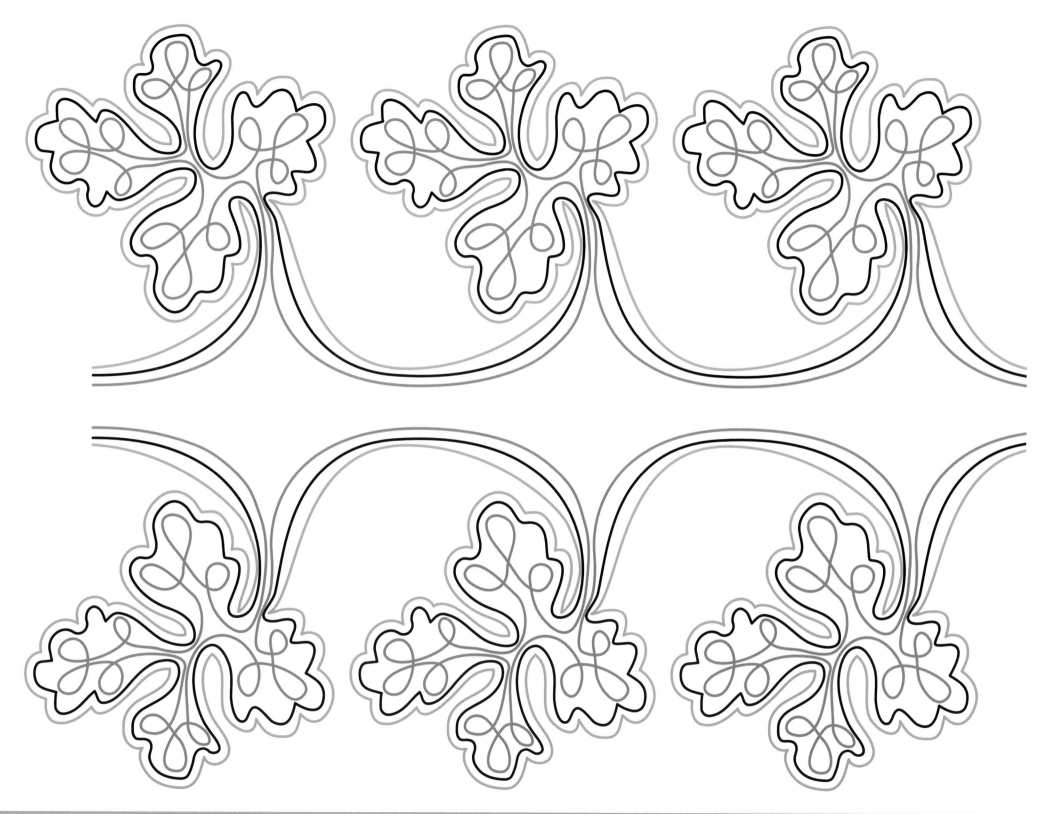

FOUR TO GO
Quadruple Line Quilting

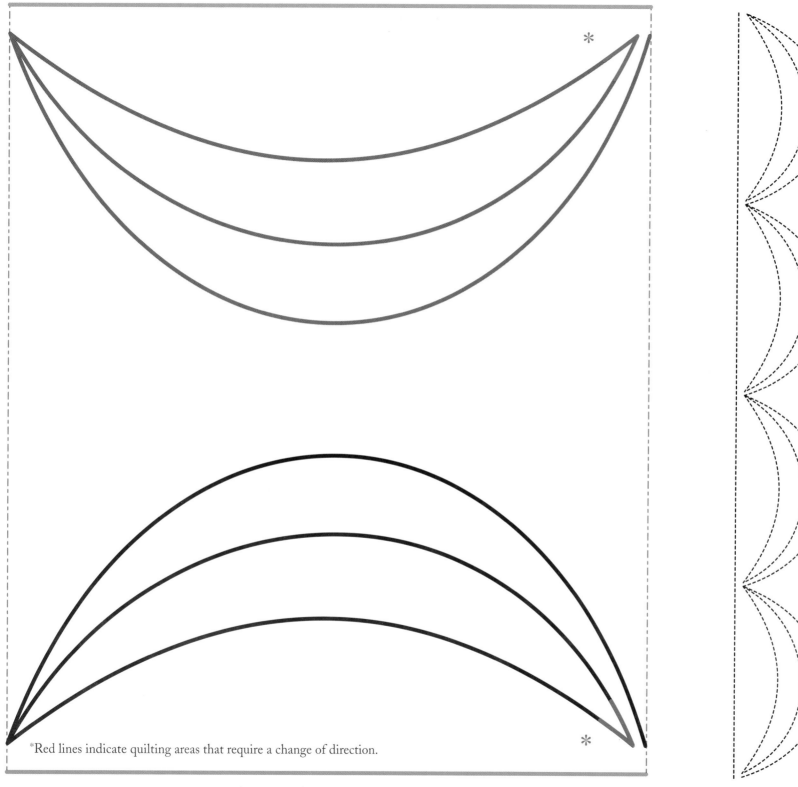

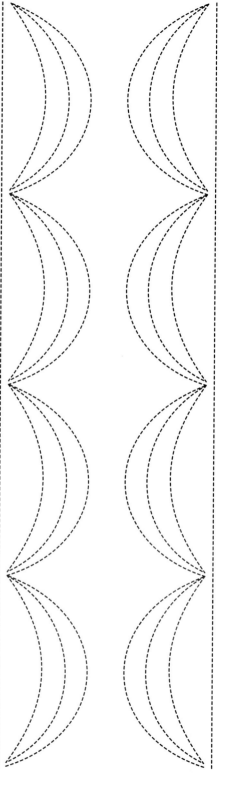

*Red lines indicate quilting areas that require a change of direction.

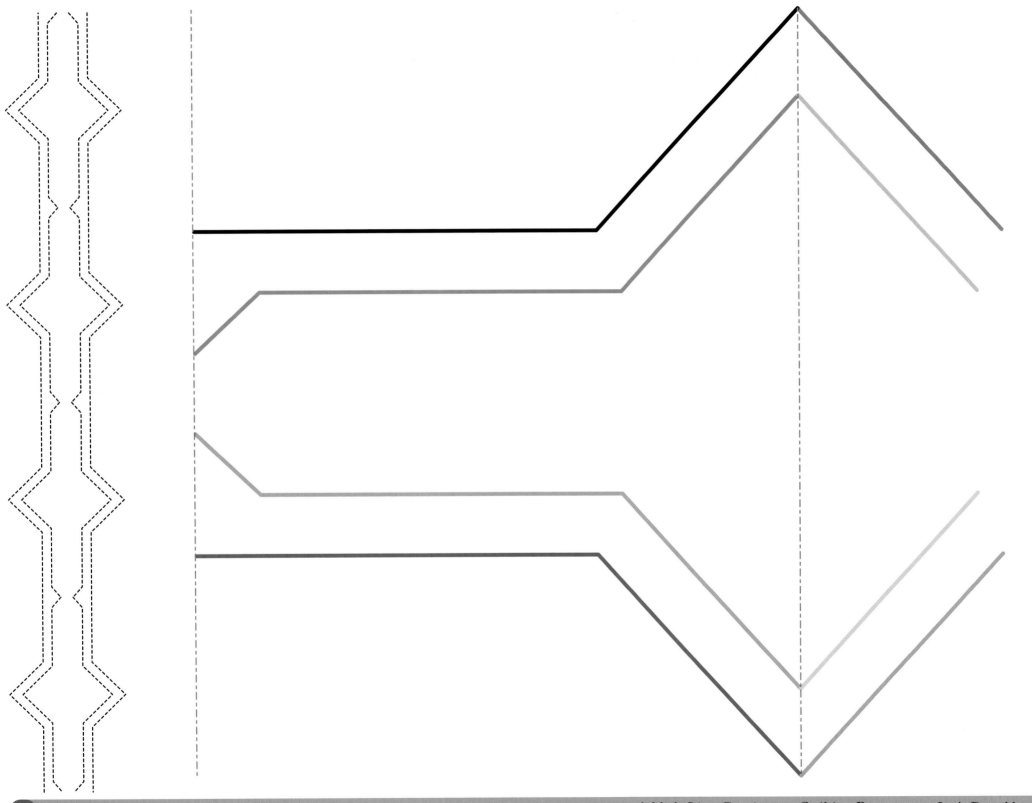

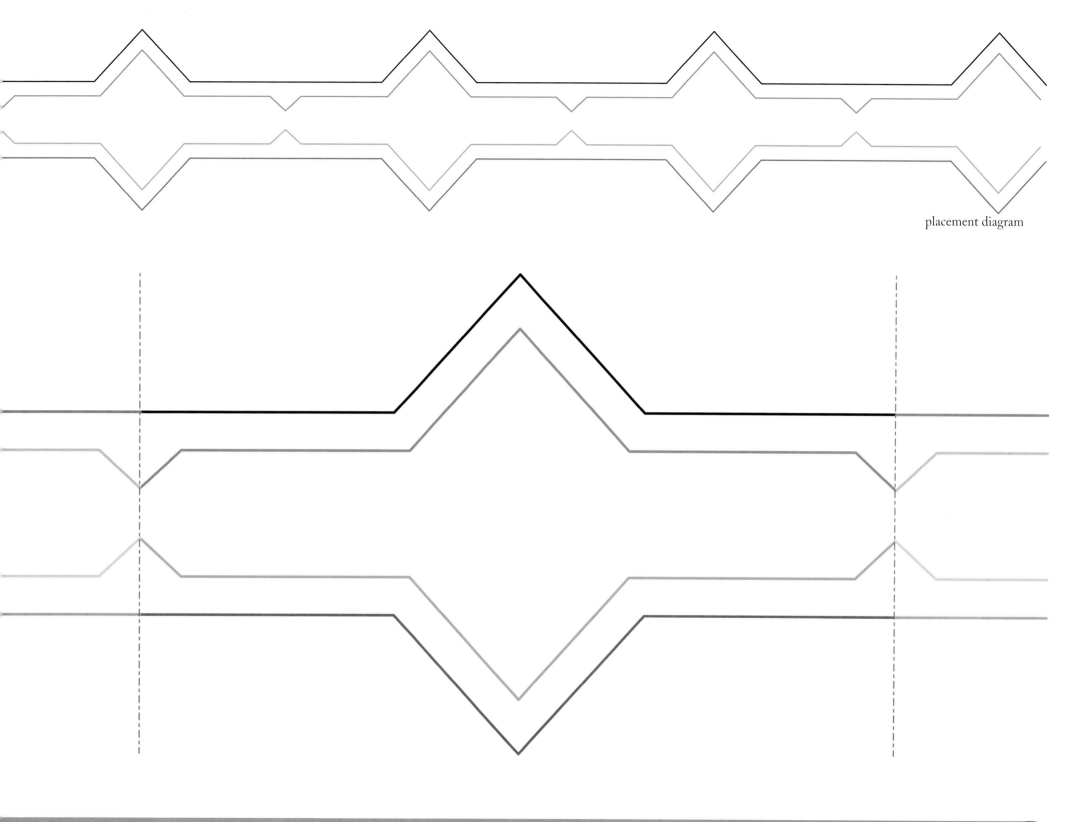

placement diagram

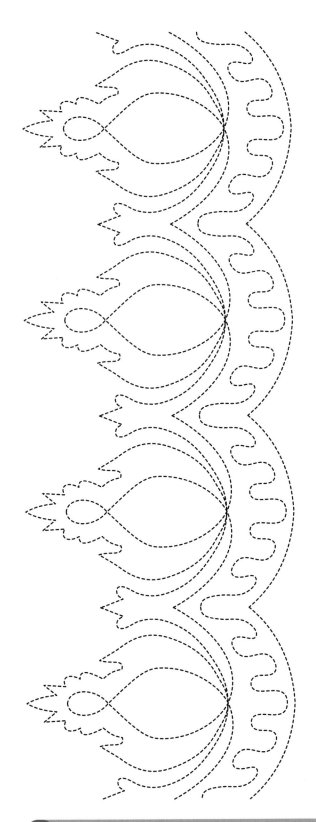

placement diagram

placement diagram

Add-A-Line Continuous Quilting Patterns — *Janie Donaldson*

DISCOVER DESIGN

Create Your Own Quilting Patterns

Discover Designs, with their predetermined positioning, are significantly easier to use than pantographs that have to be drawn from scratch. The math is already done for you!

The solid black path represents the sewing and connecting line from design to design. The red dotted line represents the area where a theme pattern is placed. The same design can be repeated or combined with other motifs as long as it fits within the area.

If you love to customize your patterns, you will enjoy this quick method of creativity, using the sixteen different Discover Design connectors on the following pages.

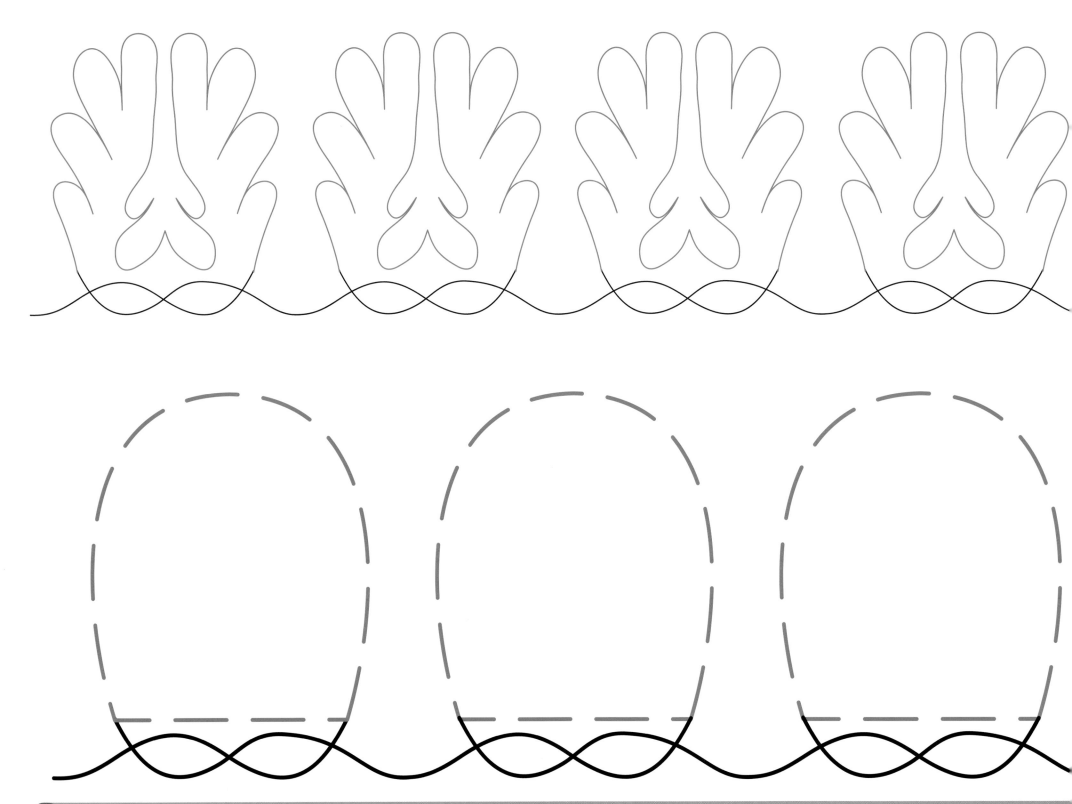

Add-A-Line Continuous Quilting Patterns — *Janie Donaldson*

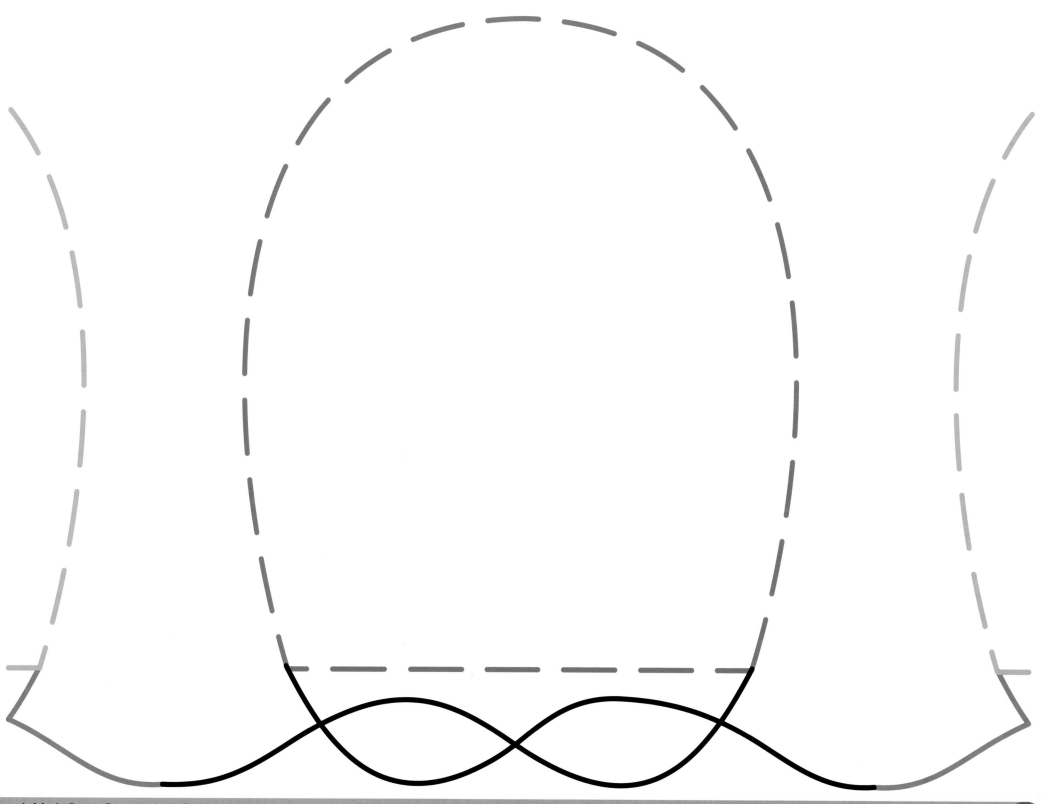

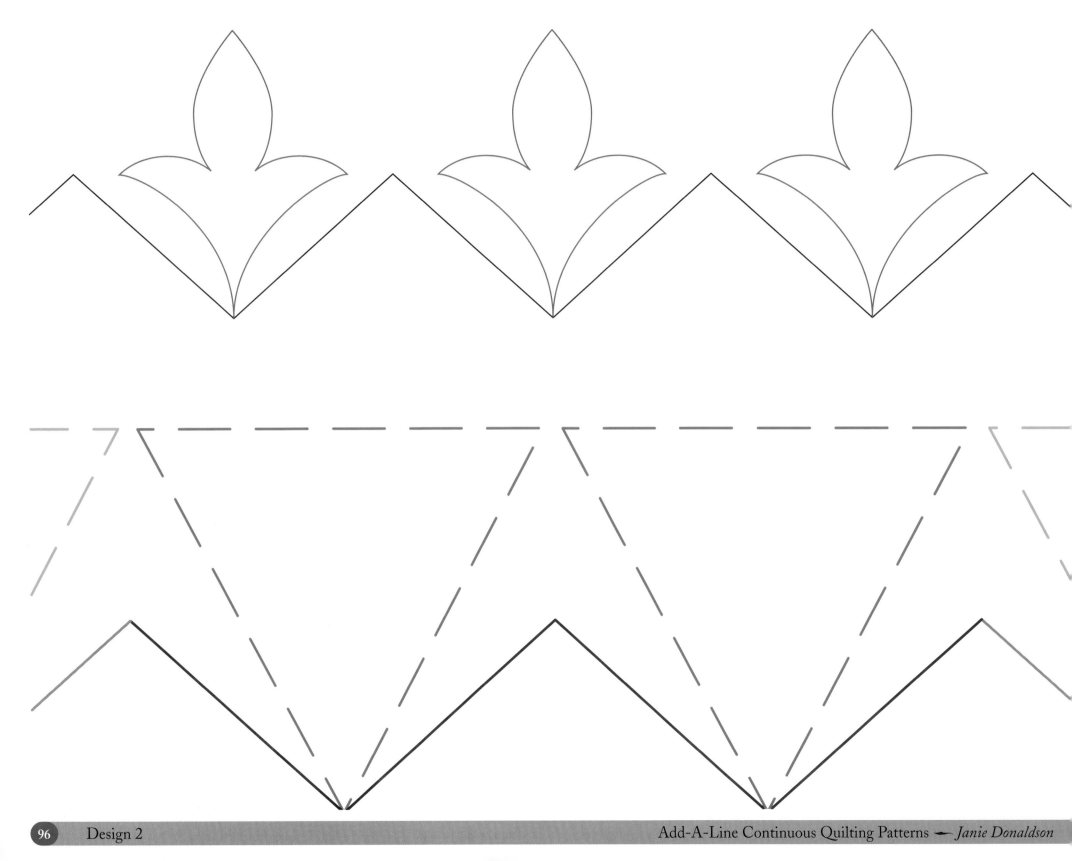

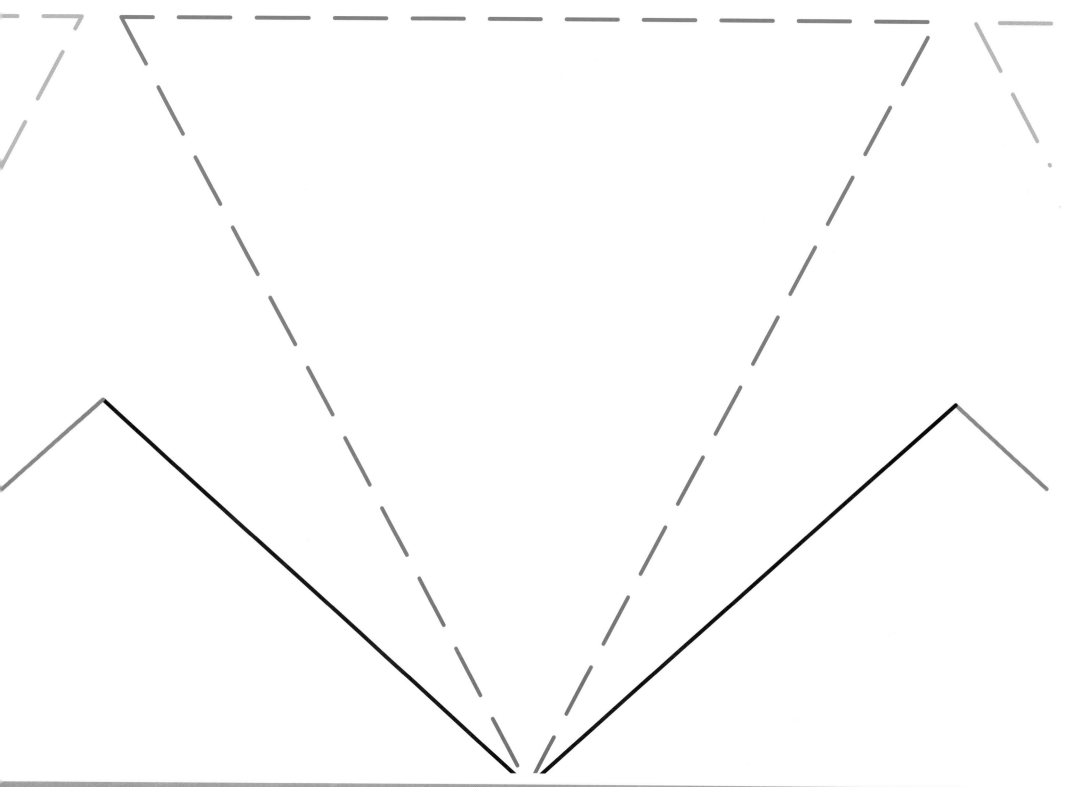

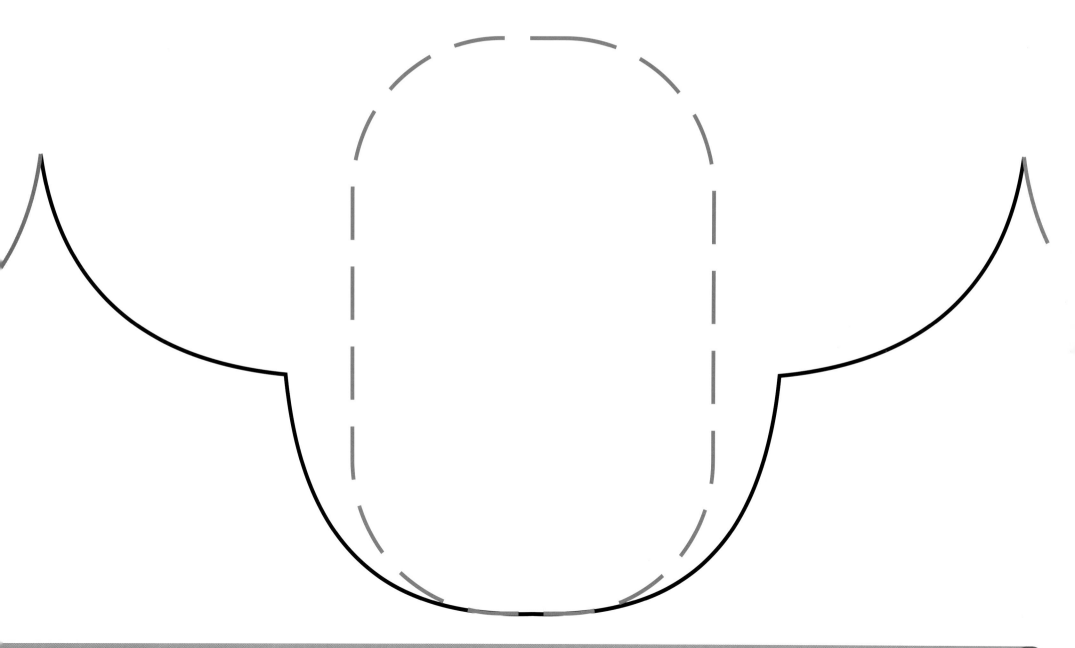

Add-A-Line Continuous Quilting Patterns — *Janie Donaldson*

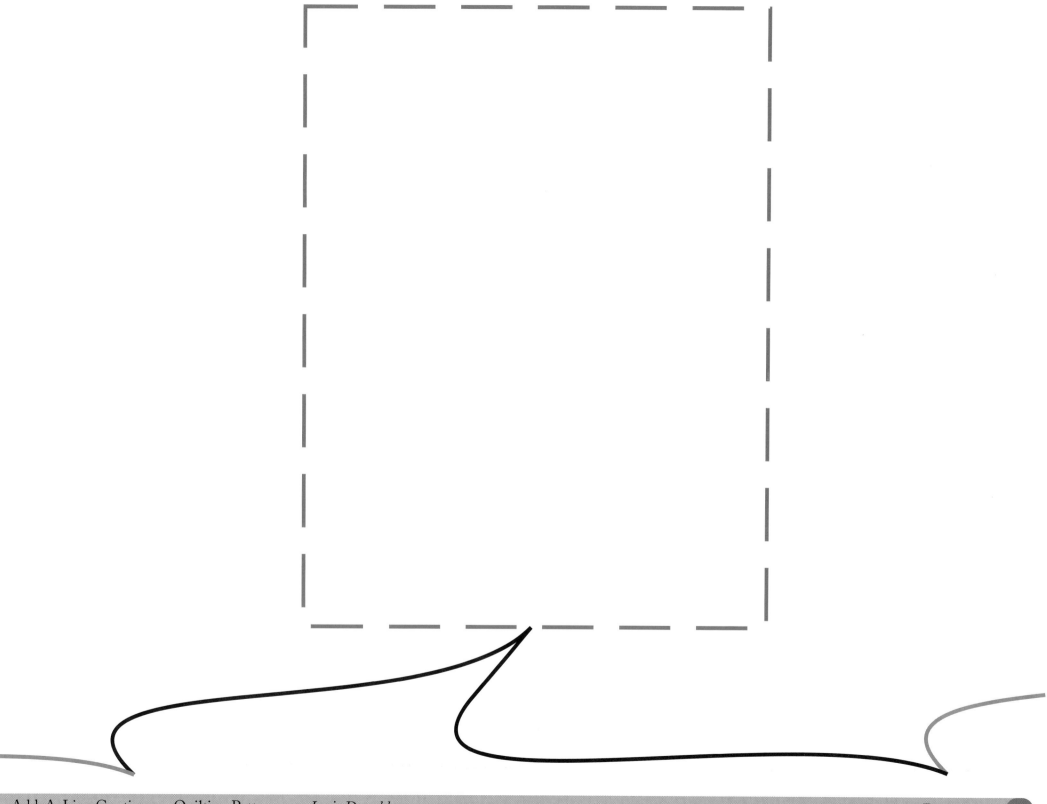

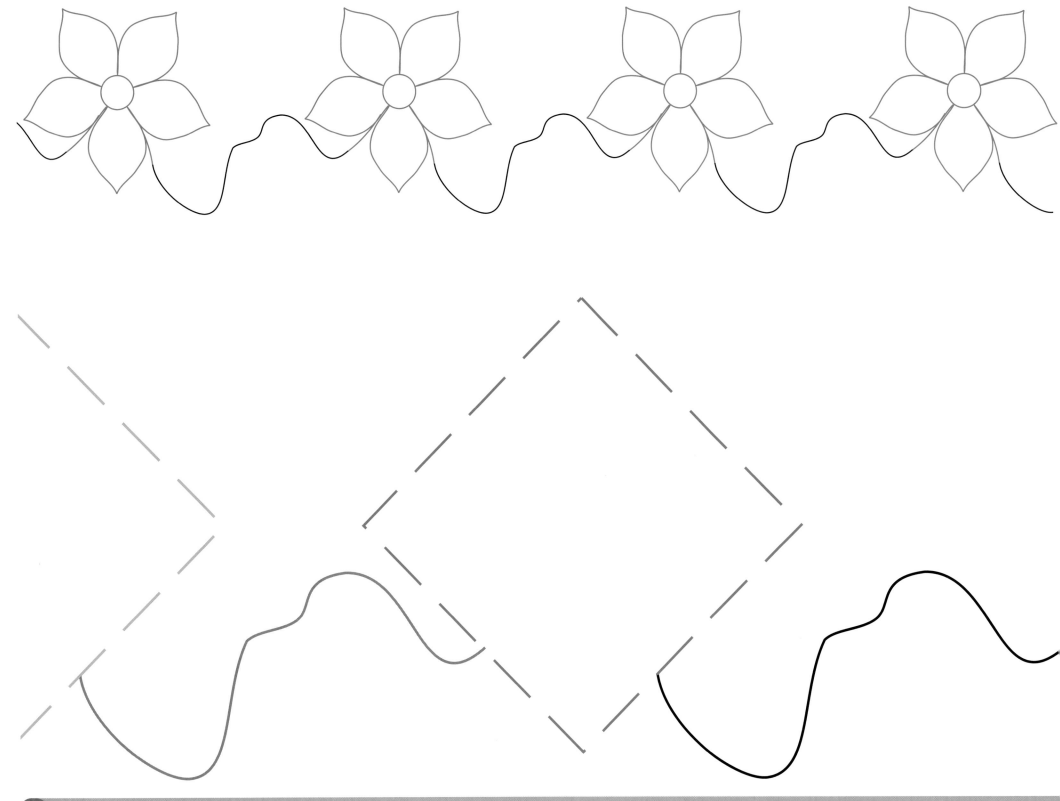

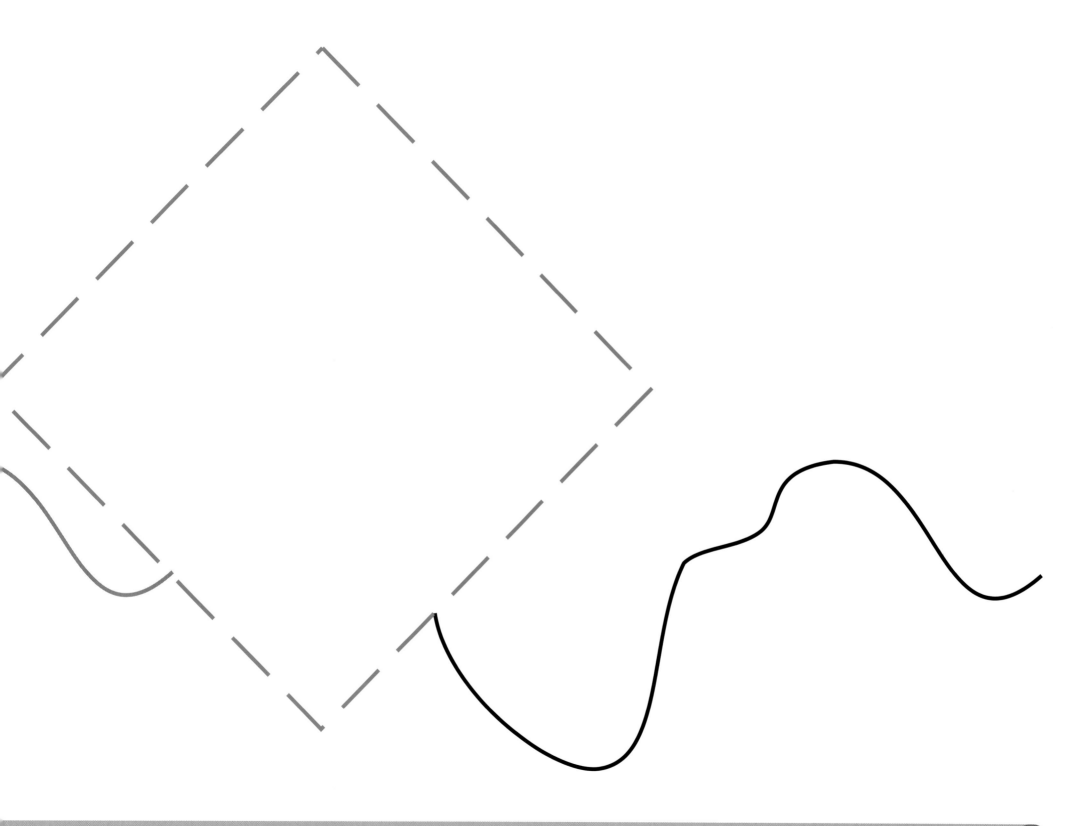

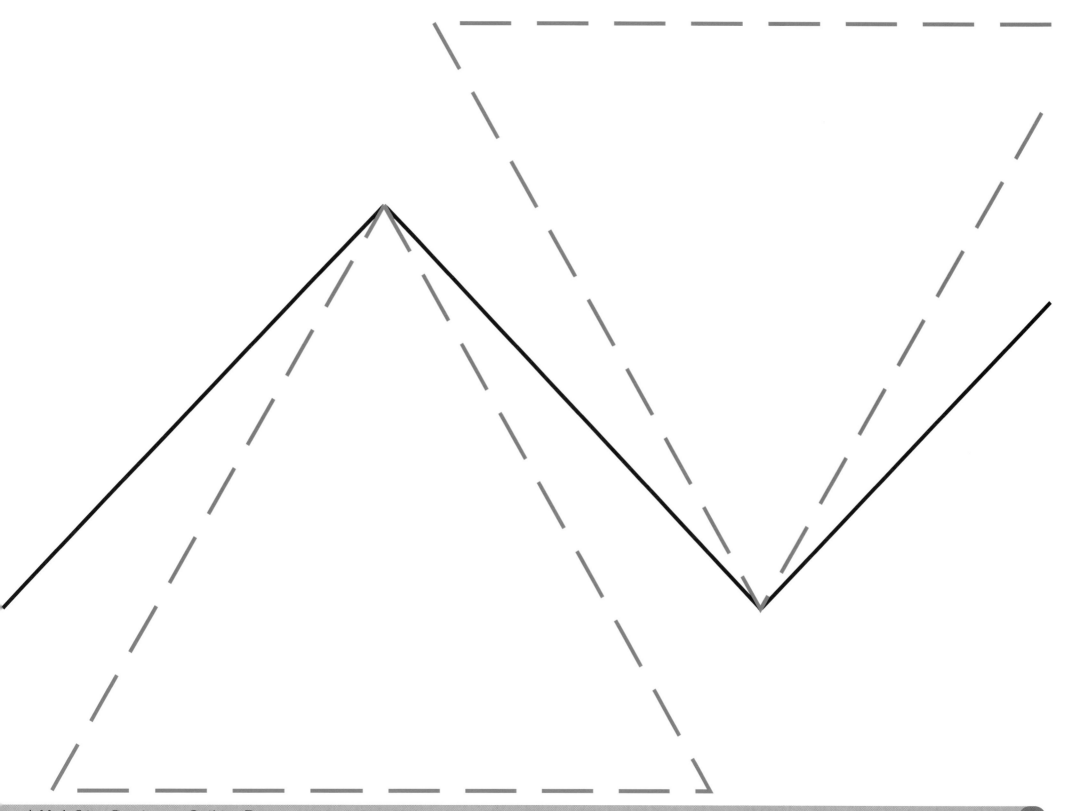

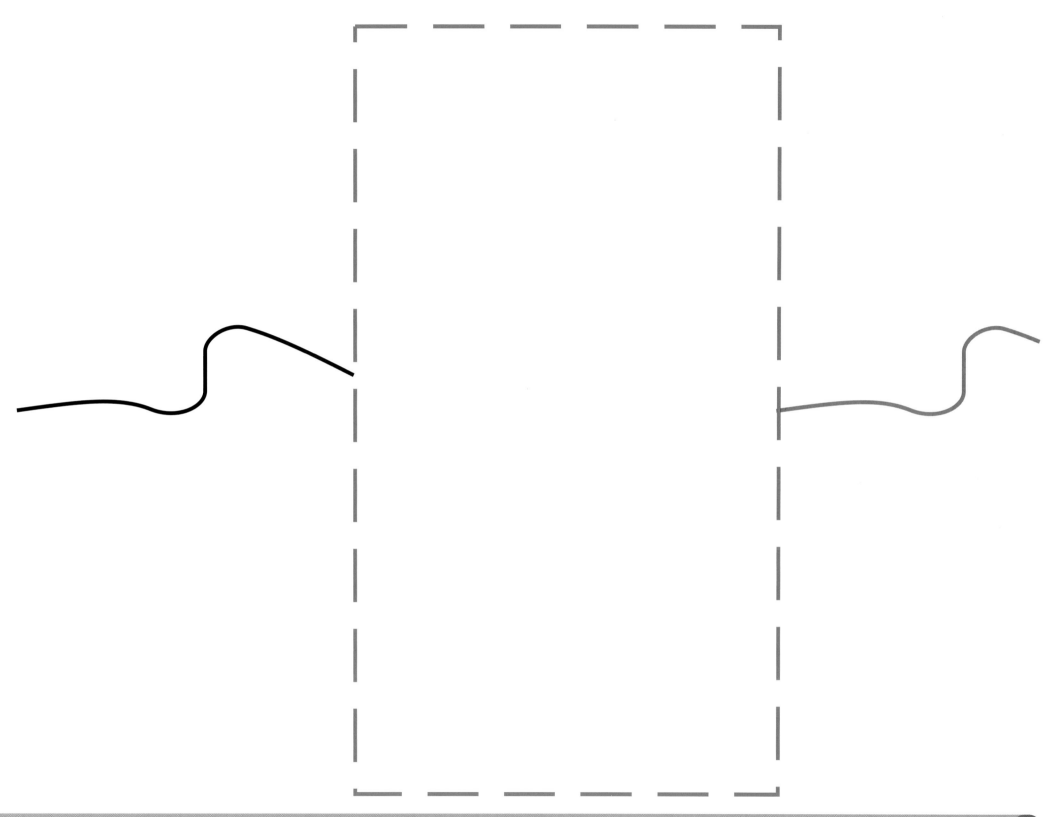

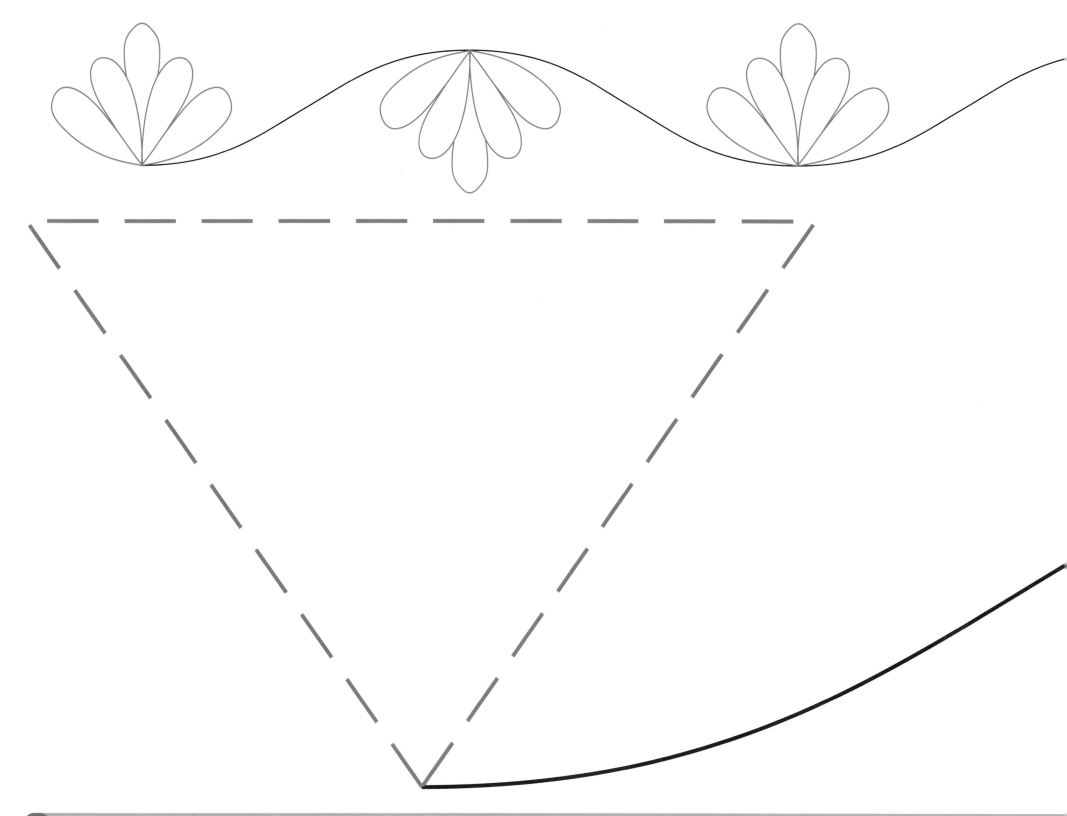

Add-A-Line Continuous Quilting Patterns — *Janie Donaldson*

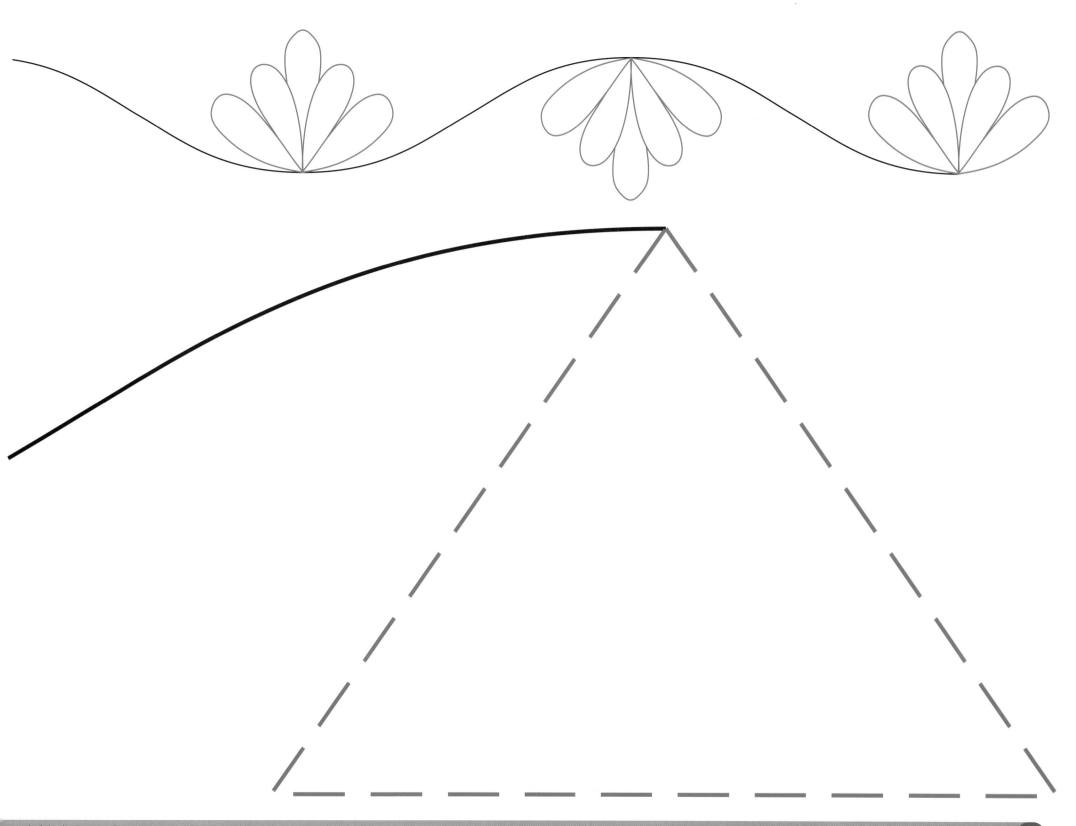

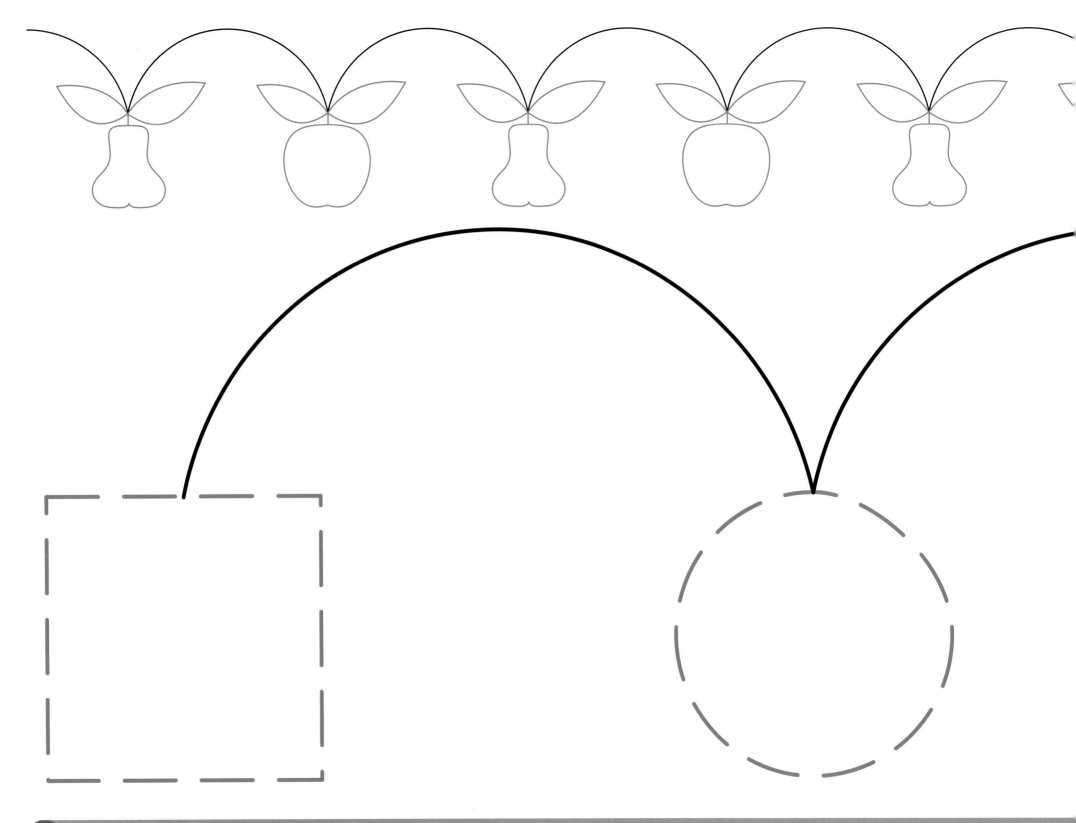

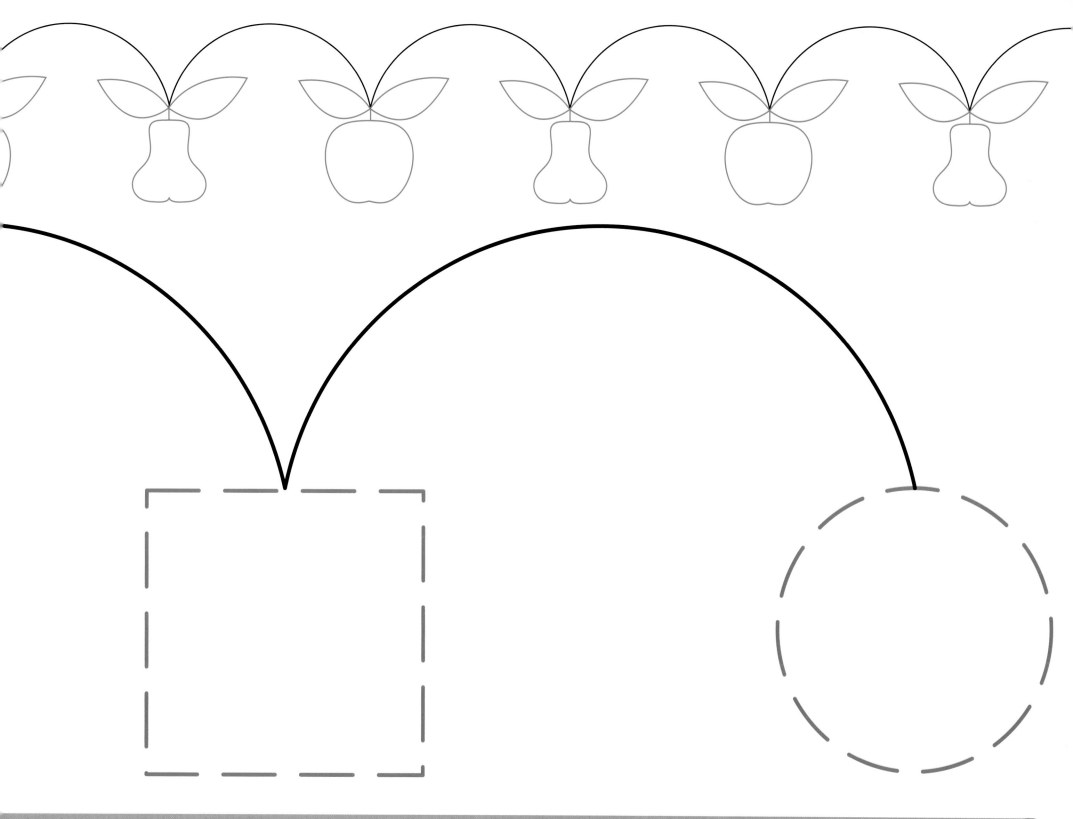

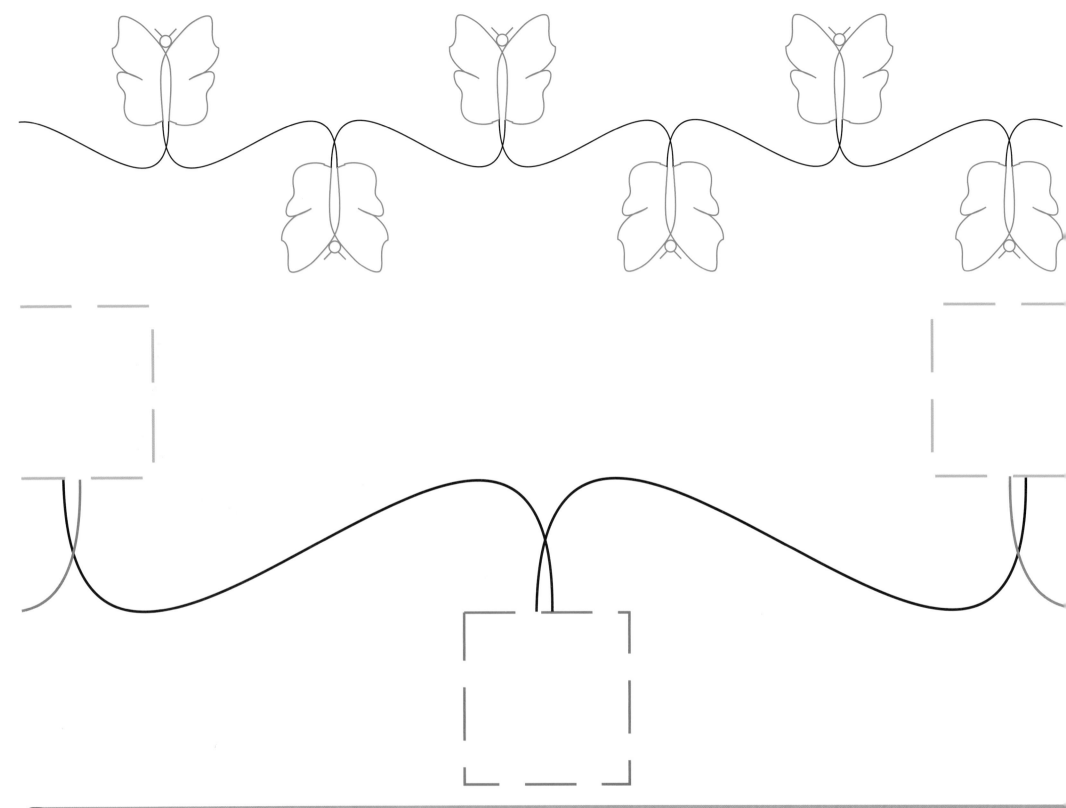

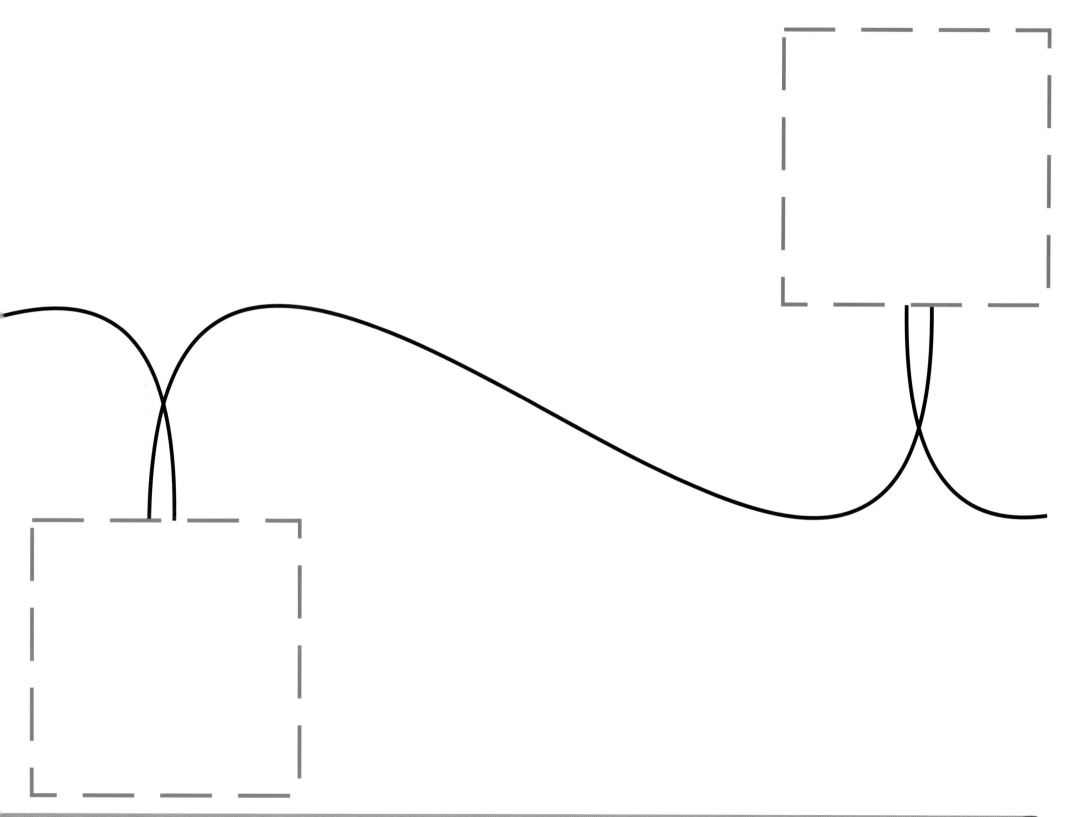

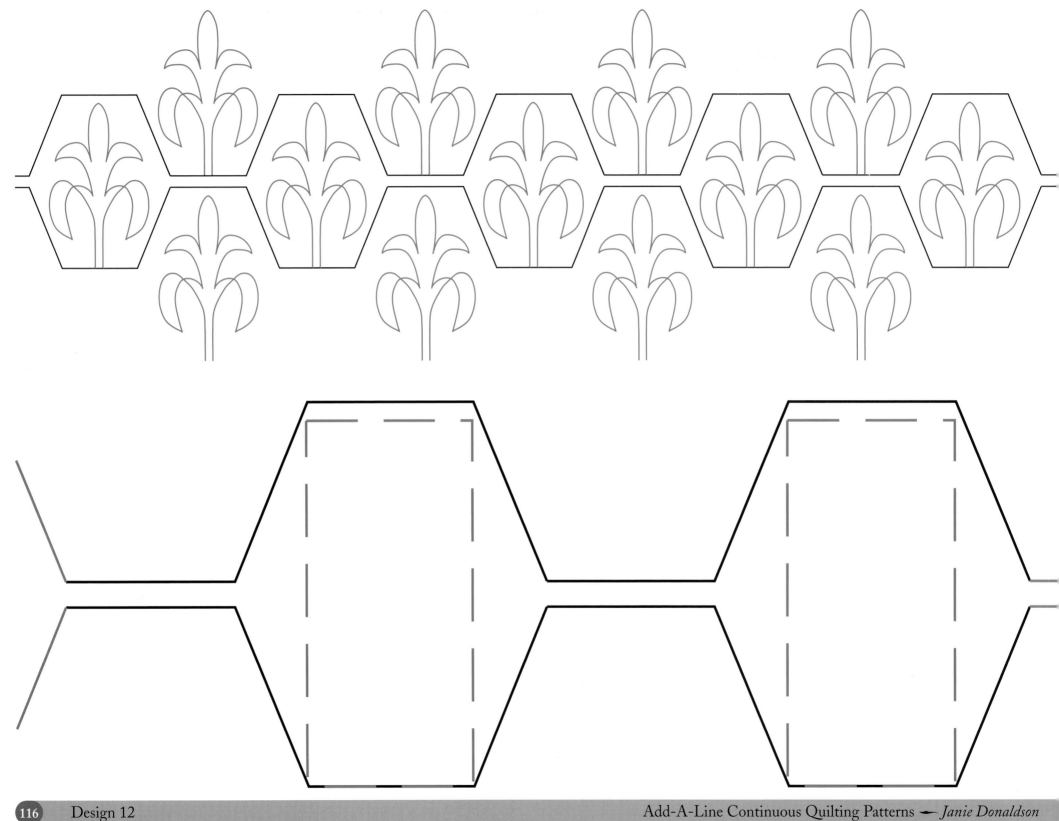

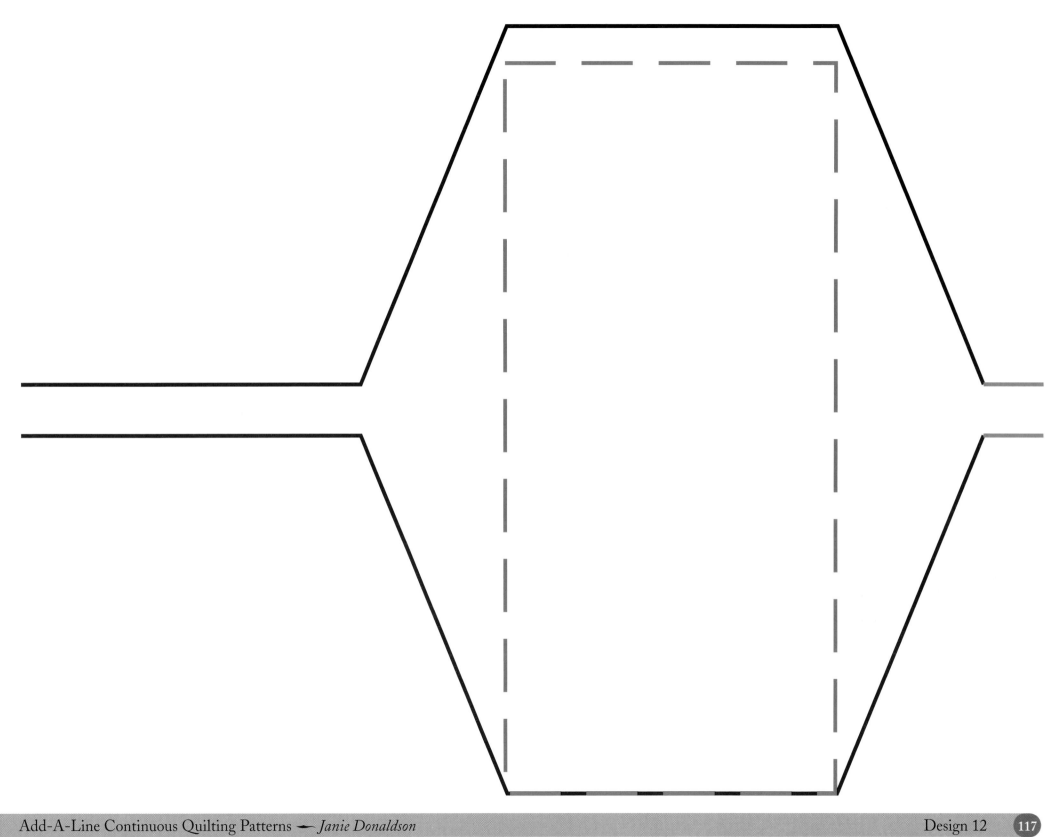

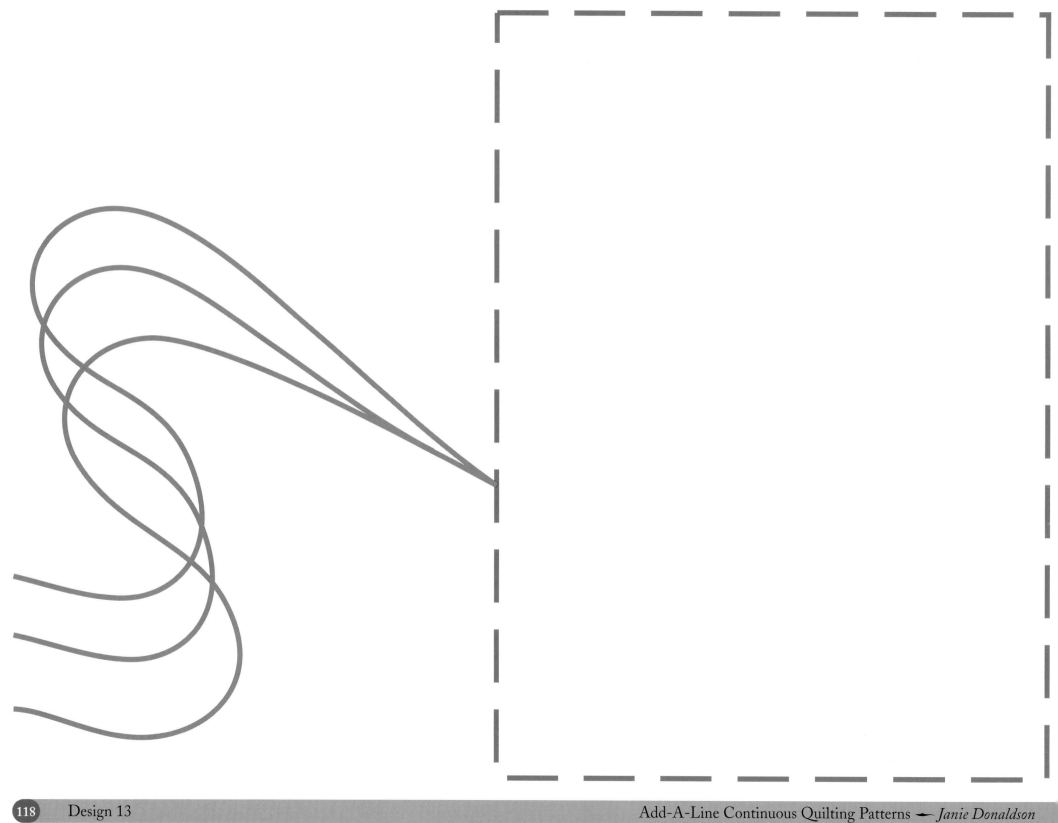

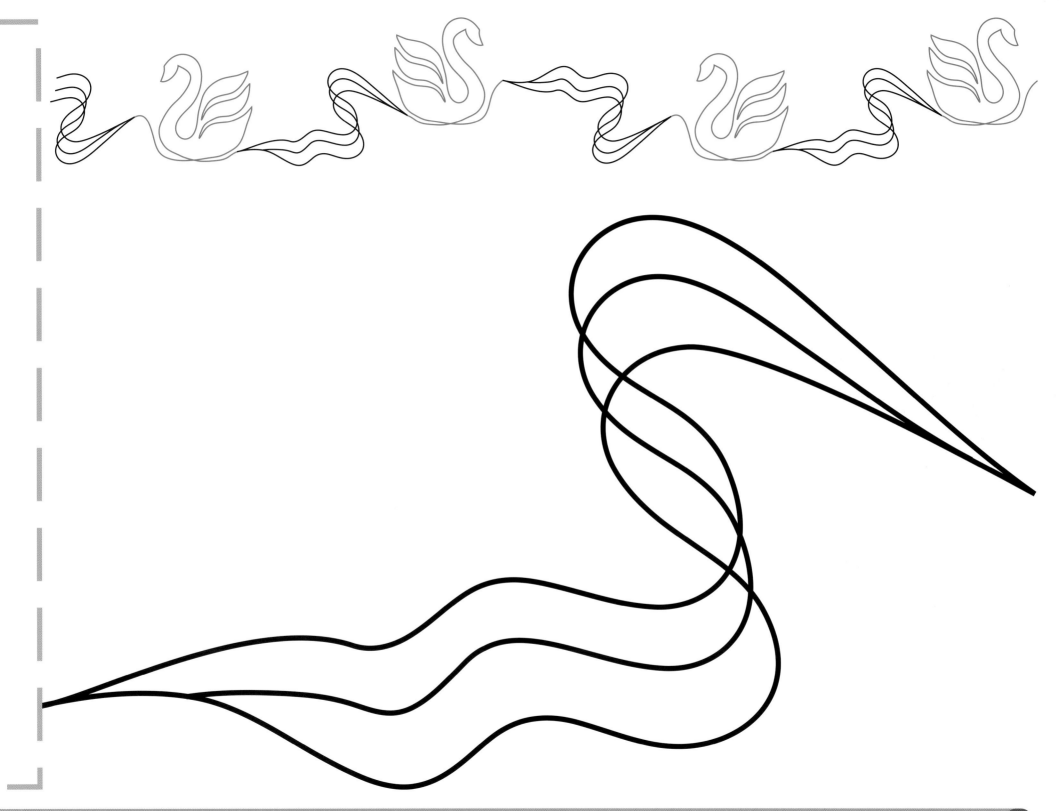

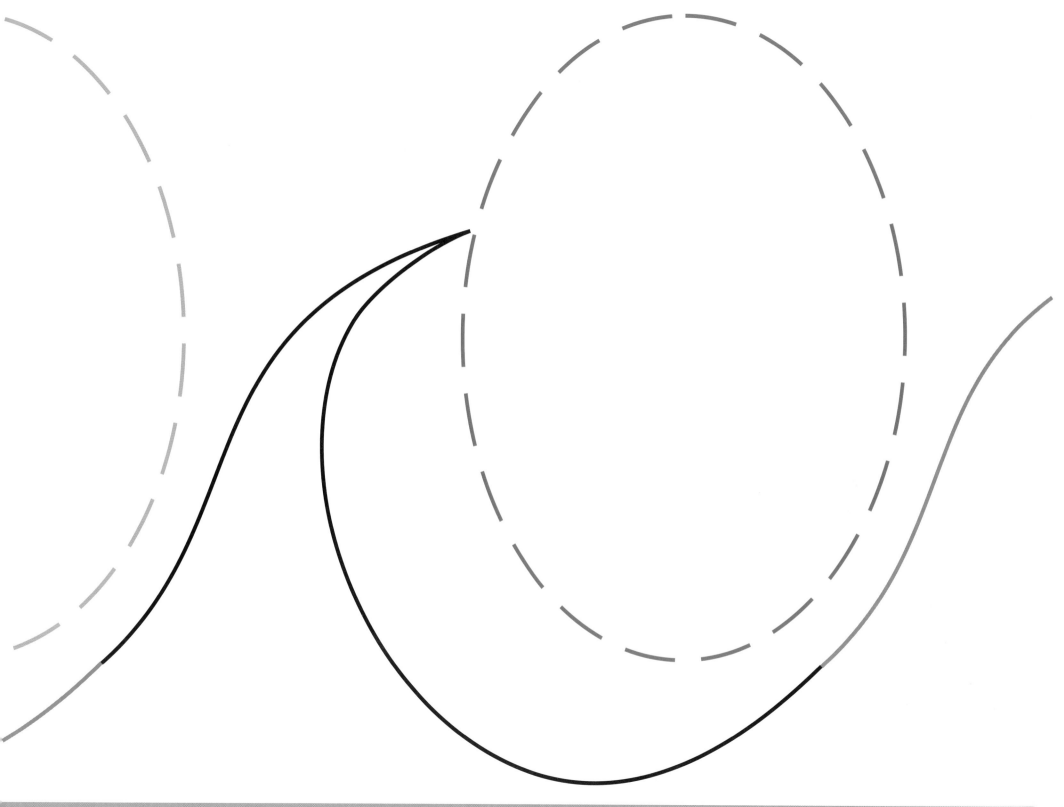

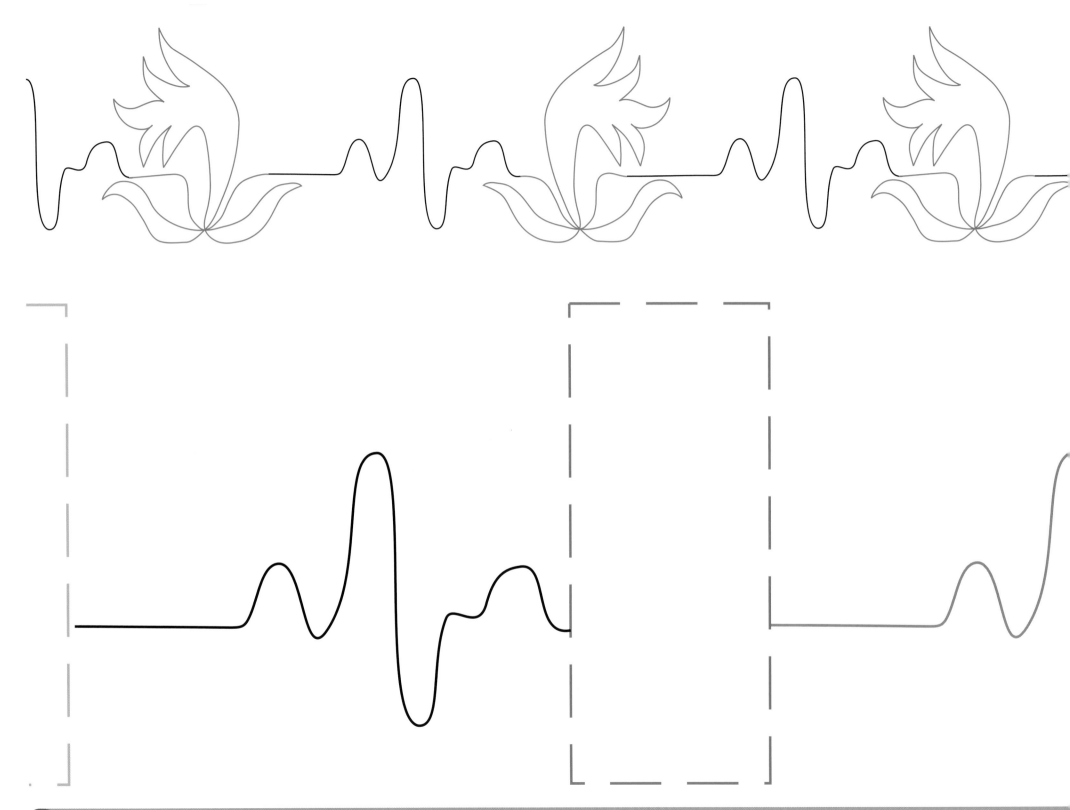

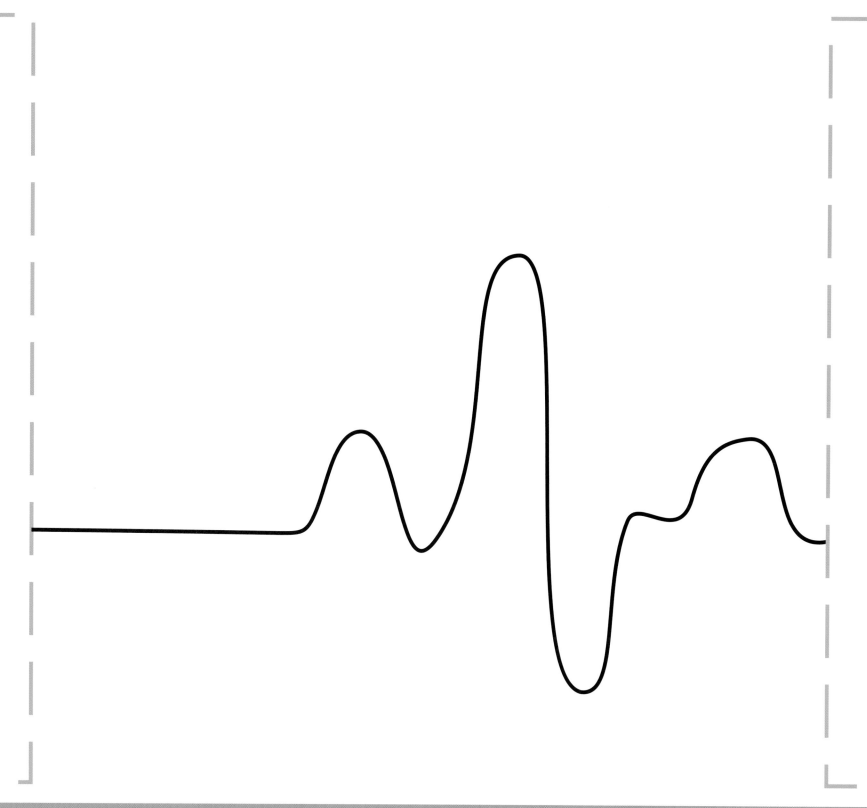

Add-A-Line Continuous Quilting Patterns — *Janie Donaldson*

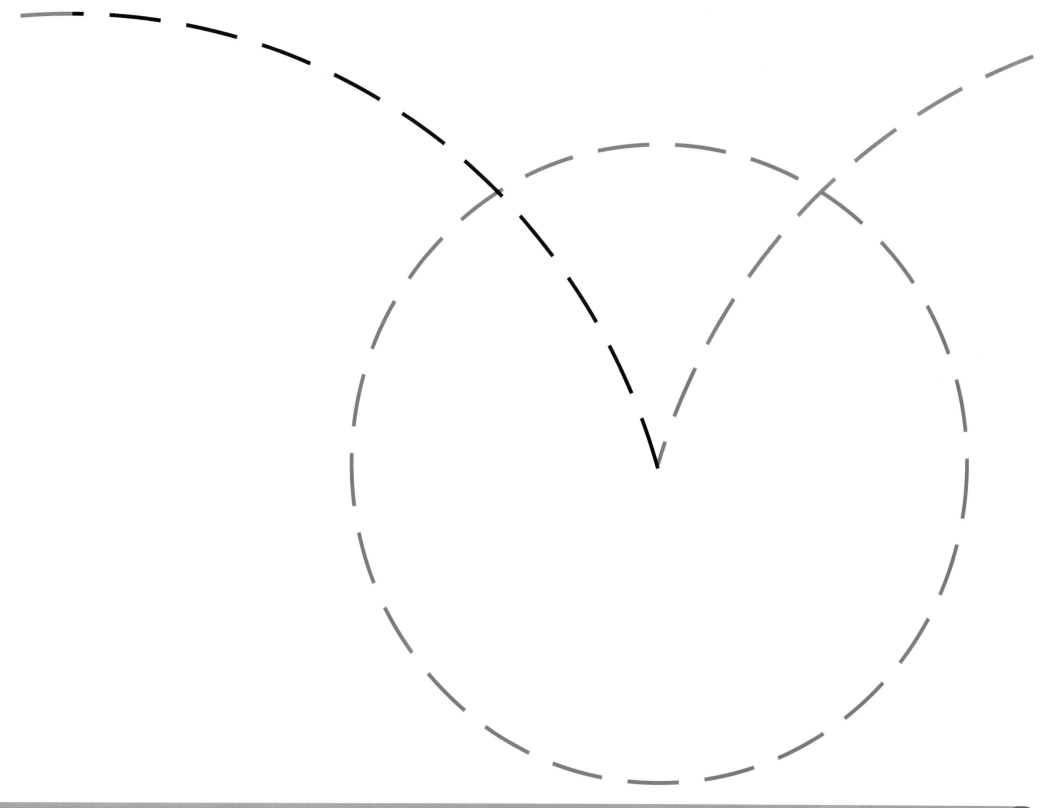

Add-a-Line Gallery

Block, Border & Corner Combinations

Add more excitement with your quilting design by using another layer of fabric! *Cut-down* and remove for a reverse appliqué effect, *cut-away* the background fabric to emphasize the main color and pattern motif.

Other exciting additions include: fraying the cut edges; sparkling sequins; colorful, variegated threads; batiks; and reproduced hand-dyed fabrics like COLOR CONNECTORS by Free Spirit, Inc.

Every pattern can be mitered to make blocks and borders. I like to elaborate the patterns at the corners as it adds extra interest to the quilting.

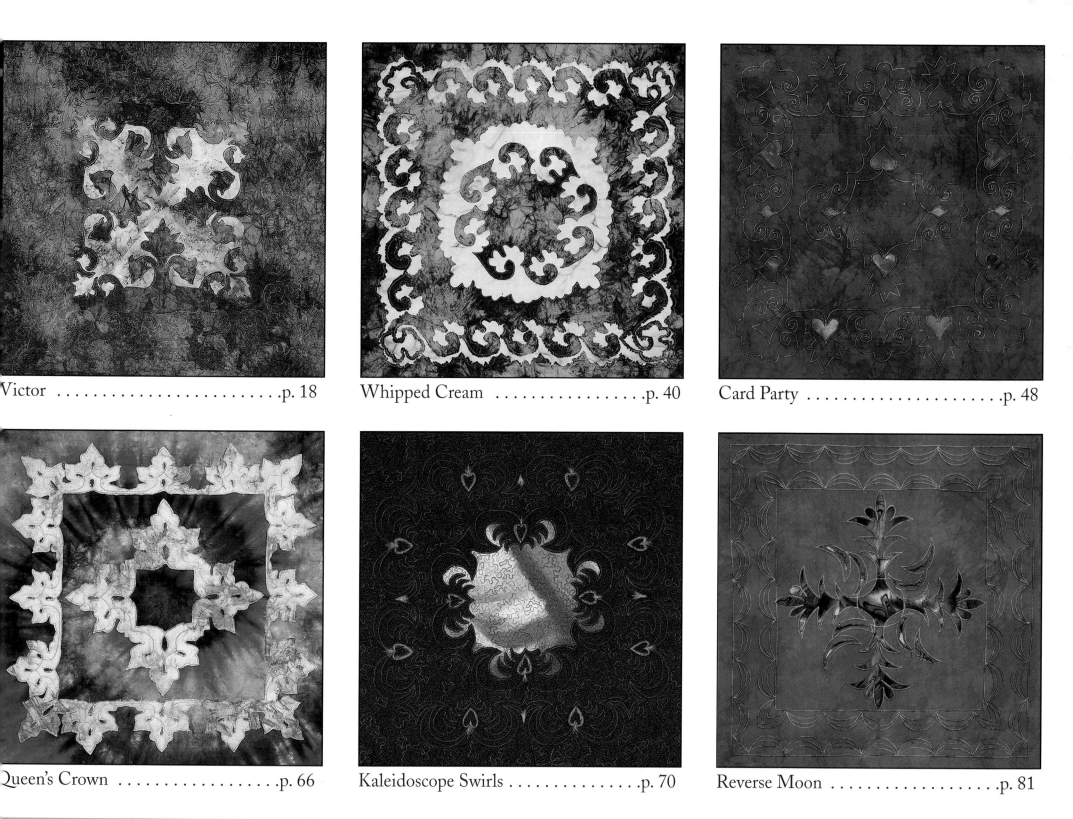

Other AQS Books

#5235   US$18.95

#5849   US$21.95

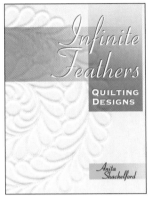

#6072   US$25.95

#4628   US$16.95

#6006   US$25.95

#2099   US$14.95

#5298   US$16.95

#6099 CD-ROM
US$29.95

#5817   US$16.95

Look for these books nationally or call *1-800-626-5420*